Dear Cecil

Jesus has given me many words to pen for a wide range of readers. However it would require the ability to write in tongues to express how each of you has helped our Lord create J. Grathmore Stratus III, in order to pen this study. I hope you enjoy this easy read, and that God speaks to you while reading, as He did to me while it was researched and patched together.

Thanks so much, and
I love you both dearly . . .

J.G.S. III
(a.k.a. Tim)

THE
ESTRANGED FAMILY
OF
ABRAHAM'S GOD

THE
ESTRANGED FAMILY
OF
ABRAHAM'S GOD

J. GRATHMORE STRATUS III

NASB – New American Standard Bible

Scripture taken from the New American Standard Bible®, Copyright © 1960, 1962, 1963, 1968, 1971, 1972, 1973, 1975, 1977, 1995 by The Lockman Foundation. Used by permission."
(www.Lockman.org)

To order additional copies of this book, contact:
Xlibris LLC
1-888-795-4274
www.Xlibris.com
Orders@Xlibris.com
550023

CONTENTS

ACKNOWLEDGMENTS

This study is dedicated to the God of Abraham, who makes all things possible, and His perfect plan for reconciliation with Him. Eternal gratitude is extended first to Him, along with thanks to Tim Foran, who allowed Alzheimer's disease to humble him to an intimate relationship with God; to Audrey Foran, who made sure her son began an intimate relationship with God the moment he was old enough to understand; to Father Wagner of St. Mark's Episcopal Church, Islip, New York (circa 1966), for his engaging and life-applicable sermons; to the many Arabian and other Middle Eastern people who extended kindness to this author while employed in their respective countries; to Paul Foran for his key role in bringing this author back to God; to Maggie Bruning for bringing this author to a God-fearing assembly; to Al and Mary Bruning for their forgiveness and faithfulness; to Palmer Olsen, Martin Fromm, and Greg Silverman for their dedication to the family of Abraham's God; to Molly Olsen, who brought Palmer into this author's life and stood alongside Palmer all those years; to Dr. Cedrick D. Brown for his *pit bullish* commitment to (and example of) living for God and tending to the needs of others before attending to the needs of his own, and Lisa and their children (Josh, Jessica, and Jaime) who make it possible for Cedrick to set the example; to Larry Lewis, who always wants an update on studies comparing the major religions; to the publishers, who have worked so hard to put this study in the hands of the readers; and to all who God desires reconciled back to Him. God make His face to shine upon them all, forever and ever. Amen.

"This mystery has not been revealed to me for any wisdom residing in me more than in any other living man, but for the purpose . . . that you may understand the thoughts of your mind" (Daniel 2:30).[1]

"This Quran has been revealed . . . that . . . it . . . may warn you" (Surah 6:91).[2]

---

[1] *New American Standard Bible*, bilingual ed. (Anaheim, CA: Foundation Publications, 1960).

[2] M. H. Shakir, trans., *Concordance of The Qur'an* (Elmhurst, NY: Tahrike Tarsile Qur'an, 2005).

INTRODUCTION

For many readers born and raised in the United States of America (USA), it may seem that if they had been placed in a time capsule as a child and not released until today, they might think they had been displaced to a distant planet. Many of them already comment on how the United States of today is not the United States they grew up in. Consider some recent observations:

> Dr. Larry Spargimino stated that "a growing number of the intellectual elite are blaming most, if not all, of our problems on religion. Christianity is, according to them, the number one culprit. Faith, they say, is dangerous. To them, only atheism avoids faith, fanaticism, and the mayhem that religion has caused the human race."[3]

> As reported by Jerry Tyson, "On June 1, 2008, Obama said in a posted YouTube video, 'Whatever we once were, we're no longer a Christian nation.'"[4]

---

[3] Larry Spargimino, "The Hostile Religion of Atheism," *Prophetic Observer* vol. 18 (October 2011): 4.

[4] Jerry Tyson, "Vatican Shake-Up—World Wake-Up," *Prophetic Observer* vol. 20 (March 2013): 2.

Noah W. Hutchings recorded that "according to a *World Net Daily* article on April 5, 2013, 'Soldiers in the U.S. military have been told in a training briefing that evangelical Christians are the No. 1 extremist threat to America—ahead of groups like the Muslim Brotherhood, KKK, Nation of Islam, al-Qaeda, Hamas, and others.' President Obama has now officially included evangelical Christians on a US government list of religious extremists, as reported by Jim Hoft at the Gateway Pundit blog on June 13, 2013."[5]

The May-June 2013 issue of *World Report* printed that "*WND.com* reports: 'A leader for the Texas branch of the Council on American Islamic Relations has told a crowd . . ." If we are practicing Muslims, we are above the law of the land" said Mustafe Carroll, the executive director of the Dallas-Fort Worth CAIR branch.'" The article further observes that "Siraj Wahhaj . . . who was asked to deliver the Juma, or invocation, at the Democratic National Convention . . . once remarked, 'It is . . . our duty as Muslims to replace the US Constitution with the Quran.'"[6]

Presumably, the sources have reported truthfully and accurately. If so, then very deep-rooted attitudes seem to be reflected in these reports. Is it possible that they are what fuel the hostilities that seem to dominate today's media? Trends of both increasing frequency and increasing severity can be readily documented by anyone willing to take the time. It can be as simple as watching the news media from one day to the next. If visiting from another planet, it might appear as though Earth was inhabited by one very large, dysfunctional

[5] Noah W. Hutchings, "A Letter from the Pastor" (Bethany, OK: Southwest Radio Ministries, July 2013);
Jack Van Impe, "World Report," *Perhaps Today* (Troy, MI: JVI Ministries, May-June 2013).

[6] Jack Van Impe, "World Report," *Perhaps Today* (Troy, MI: JVI Ministries, May-June 2013).

family. This study presents considerations that seem to be overlooked by many authors attempting to analyze ancient rivalries that continue to shape the history of mankind.

It is hoped that anyone anguished by estranged family relations will benefit from this study, regardless of attitudes or beliefs. However, it does spend time examining a view from what are commonly accepted to be the three major Abrahamic religions. The existence of a fourth is respectfully recognized. There are many different sections within each respective system. What is considered common to all sections within each respective system is the subject of ongoing debates. The readers or listeners can investigate this breakdown on their own. It is not this author's intention to convince anyone in the matter of faith or to judge their religion or belief system. The use of capital *G* in *God* in this book refers to the God of Abraham, in which the Abrahamic religions claim to be rooted. As it should be, the readers remain free to draw their own conclusions. A presentation of facts and questions is aimed at helping each reader to formulate the most informed conclusion possible. The God of Abraham does not need any assistance from the author to prove that He exists or to explain everything about Him. This study is not commissioned for that purpose.

If Christianity is indeed the culprit for all our problems as mentioned, and America's founding fathers based the law of the land upon Judeo-Christian principles, then law based on the Qur'an might be an alternative to consider. One must be fully informed before considering something so critical. All three of these major faith systems claim ancestry back to Abraham. So why is there so much tension in that family? Why has Abraham's family become estranged? Which major religion's values should propel the law of the land? Can all three major religions reconcile and follow one moral standard with a universal peace of mind? Do possible solutions need to start at the individual household level? Can success at the household level extend into neighborhoods and ultimately improve the quality of life in communities? Is there any hope a solution can foster world peace? The essence of these questions will be objectively explored in the chapters that follow.

Preserving an objective view in this writing includes the side-by-side bilingual English with Arabic, or Hebrew or Greek language reference sources, as appropriate. This is especially true regarding the holy and sacred writings of each respective faith. By way of example, page 8 of the preface to Al-Qur'an states, "This is . . . a translation and not an interpretation, theological or otherwise, therefore, closest to the original in meaning . . . of Arabic words," while page 7 states, "The form of metrical lines has . . . been adopted in this translation to convey through accent, sprung rhythm and tonal structure the sonority and rhythmic patterns of the Qur'anic language."[7] In similar fashion, Michael Sells points out that in Surah 55, "The Arabic original contains an incantatory rhythmic intensity . . . In contrast to English, Arabic grammar allows a natural, unobtrusive expression of the dual through the forms of verbs and pronouns . . . tying that core message into the morphology and the acoustics of the language . . . the theme of twos unfolds through enigmatic and lyrical signs of creative bounty."[8]

J. Grathmore Stratus III hopes to equip each reader to formulate their own conclusion(s) from as informed a position as is possible. The author makes no claim(s) to agree or disagree with anything found in the bibliography. The opinions of the author do not matter. The only conclusion that matters is the one that each respective reader formulates according to his or her own accountability.

---

[7]   Ahmed Ali, *AL-QUR'AN*, bilingual ed. (Princeton, NJ: Princeton University Press, 1993).

[8]   Michael Sells, *Approaching the Quran*, 2nd ed. (Ashland, OR: White Cloud, 1999).

CHAPTER ONE

WHAT MAKES A FAMILY?

Perhaps the one thing everyone might agree on is that nobody is perfect, including J. Grathmore Stratus III. Chances are that even a person who might disagree with this probably has family members and friends who are imperfect. Typically, everyone has their patience and peace of mind challenged by the imperfections of others. Therefore, it would be difficult to find anyone who would not benefit from exploring this book.

It is common knowledge that every infant is born helpless and requires some form of human interaction. That interaction begins to shape how the infant responds to any subsequent human contact. Ordinarily, that subsequent human contact unfolds in the family environment. If not family by flesh and blood, then by some substitute form provided by social services or charity. Either way, everyone starts their life journey helpless. Lack of breath would quickly suffocate any infant without the slap on its backside. No one can survive if they are abandoned upon delivery from the womb. Infant survival requires intimate contact. The tenderness of nursing and changing diapers are simple examples. Every infant shares that common bond of helplessness and the resulting need for intimacy. Soon they encounter other toddlers, and they seem to get along just fine. As children grow, however, they end up divided into one or more categories that society creates. The harmony once shared with others ends up broken. Almost as if by default, children are prepared to perpetuate social, military, and political tension when they become adults. If that is the case, it would make sense that current world anxiety can be traced back to the time and place that the once-shared harmony was broken. The beginning is that point of shared helplessness and need for intimacy. This is why humility is vital in displacing pride. Imagine if an infant was too proud to be smacked on the backside and prevented the doctor from doing so. Because that is not possible, then imagine if the mother was too proud to have her infant smacked on the backside? Mankind is introduced to humility immediately at birth. It leads to the intimacy of human relations. This, in turn, leads to life! It is the cornerstone of family. So then, what does *family* look like?

From the Latin word *familia*, family refers to people grouped according to common origin, ancestry, kinship, or genetics as well as marriage, adoption, and close relationships. Family is also considered an institution from the viewpoint of law, history, and demography. Reproduction, daily sustenance, nurturing care, safety, behavioral development, and following moral standards are the functions that are customarily expected of a family. Some anthropologists propose that many societies define *kinship* differently.[9] That argument is reserved for the authoritative books already written on the subject.

For sake of simplicity, this writing accepts the commonly used terms such as *father, mother, brother, sister, grandparent, uncle, aunt, cousin, nephew, niece, stepbrother/stepsister, in-law,* and any related adoptions. According to Michael Lamb, PhD, "Parents will help children grow and learn valuable life lessons. There is great importance of communication . . . in families."[10] It is preferred that love, trust, intimacy, and tenderness are included. A family member can return home from work or school to escape from the aggressions

---

[9] *Wikipedia, the free encyclopedia*, s.v. "Family," accessed March 2013, https://en.wikipedia.org/wiki/Family.html.

[10] *Wikipedia, the free encyclopedia*, s.v. "Family," accessed March 2013, https://en.wikipedia.org/wiki/Family.html.

of the world. To the contrary, many return home to a broken family. Too often, concern for family members is replaced by selfish desire. In many cases, one of the parents is unnecessarily absent, and a child's growth is hindered. In other cases, "Many philosophers and psychiatrists . . . argue, the young develop in a perverse relationship, wherein they learn to love the same person who beats and oppresses them . . . physically or mentally . . . they will desire social repression."[11]

Another in-depth look is provided by Henry Cloud, who states, "A family can make itself a safe place for less-than-perfect people to learn . . . to . . . live in a less-than-perfect world." He continues that "as people living in a real world, we are going to have some negative feelings such as sadness, anger, and fear . . . jealousy, envy, pride, rage, lust and so on . . . The family needs to be a place where its members . . . find safe solutions for these deficiencies."

Mr. Cloud elaborates,

> When we bond and attach, our inner life abides in the life of another person . . . we "matter" to someone . . . we feel that we make a difference . . . that our presence is desired . . . and missed when we are absent.

> The family should be the very first place where its members can . . . count on . . . others to fuel their emotional needs . . . where needs for love are met . . . to go out . . . and take their place as people with purpose and mission.

> The goal is for parents to impart God's ways to the children and get them ready for independence . . . gradually to shift power from himself to the maturing child . . . families must provide the freedom

---

[11] *Wikipedia, the free encyclopedia*, s.v. "Family," accessed March 2013, https:// en.wikipedia.org/wiki/Family.html.

to fail . . . achieving adulthood is practically impossible without learning through failure.[12]

Observations such as these indicate several opportunities for a dysfunction to manifest and take root in a family. For many years, J. Grathmore Stratus III assumed the idiosyncracies observed in his family were unique only to them. However, he has listened to many people from many different races and cultures talk about their own dysfunctional family. Mr. Stratus speculates that probably every family on earth experiences an estranged family situation. Most, however, remain reluctant to admit it. Most revert back to that natural tendency to cover it up.

Dysfunctions can lead to divisions in the family purpose. The consequences can reach far into society. The three major world religions that reside in Jerusalem (and elsewhere) all trace their spiritual roots back to Abraham and his God.[13] Perhaps the perpetually mounting tensions in the Middle East are the consequence of dysfunction(s) in the family God promised to Abraham. A study of how God planned to establish His family through Abraham should provide valuable insight into restoring harmony and securing universal peace. Any study, however, would be premature without first knowing what to look for. In other words, what are the characteristics of an estranged family?

---

[12] Dave Carder et al., *Unlocking Your Family Patterns* (Chicago, IL: Moody Publishers 1991, 1993, 2011), 122, 123, 159.

[13] F. E. Peters, *The Children of Abraham* (Princeton, NJ: Princeton University Press, 2004), 21.

CHAPTER TWO

CHARACTERISTICS OF AN ESTRANGED FAMILY

It is obvious that very deep emotions and feelings can cause, and be caused by, dysfunctions in a family. Perhaps the root cause is best expressed by Bruno Giamba in his August 2013 work titled "Let's Get Real." Mr. Giamba submits that "a conscience is an inner code of conduct." He continues by showing how a feeling of guilt manifests when someone violates their inner code. Typically, a person attempts to cover up the resulting shame. "Let's Get Real" elaborates that "when we cover up, we begin creating another standard of truth . . . the feeling of guilt has been justified with the feeling of entitlement. You will often hear the rationalization statement, 'God wants me to be happy and I am not happy with my wife and happier with this other woman.' We have established our emotion of happiness as the new standard of truth."[14]

In researching to write this book, J. Grathmore Stratus III found nothing to indicate that there might be someone who lacks a sense of right from wrong. Beyond the research, fifty-nine years of life experience and global human contact have not revealed the likelihood of anyone who does not sense when they have done something wrong. At appropriate times, Dr. Cedrick Brown

---

[14] Bruno R. Giamba, "Let's Get Real" (sermon, Souderton, Pennsylvania, August 2013).

reminds folks that a child never needs to be taught what is wrong. The words *no* and *mine* seem to be two of the first three or four words children begin to speak. Children do not need to be taught how to do wrong, but parents, teachers, and society spend much of their time correcting them. This author is not able to think of, or has never heard of, any exceptions to this observation. According to the National Center for Infants, Toddlers, and Families, "The most common (and challenging) issues facing parents of babies and toddlers today are . . . Aggression, Defiance."[15] The US National Library of Medicine, National Institutes of Health confirms that "All kids misbehave . . . behavior disorders are . . . serious. They . . . include . . . Harming or threatening . . . people or pets . . . Damaging or destroying property . . . Lying or stealing, Frequent tantrums."[16] Notice here that the experts include "all kids." For that reason, it is difficult to argue that man is basically good by nature and will eventually evolve out of all the troubles mankind has caused.

Notwithstanding, "All Abrahamic religions . . . speak of a choice between good and evil . . . associated with obedience or disobedience to a single God and to Divine law."[17] The natural tendency to cover up wrongdoing is found in both the Qur'an (Islam; Sura 20:121) and the Bible (Judeo-Christian Genesis 3:7). Can a study of estrangement help identify an escape from the propensity for wrongdoing? To answer this question, the term *estrangement* needs to be defined.

In the stoic sense, academic definitions include the following:

---

[15] National Center for Infants, Toddlers, and Families. "ZERO TO THREE— Behavior & Development" (Washington, DC: September 2013), http://www.zerotothree.org/child-development/.

[16] US National Library of Medicine *NIH* National Institutes of Health, "MedlinePlus—Child Behavior Disorders," accessed September 2013, http://www.nim.nih.gov/medlineplus/childbehaviordisorders.html.

[17] *Wikipedia, the free encyclopedia*, s.v. "Abrahamic religions," accessed April 2013, http://en.wikipedia/wiki/Abrahamic_religions.htm.

e*strange*

1. To make hostile, unsympathetic, or indifferent, alienate.
2. To remove from an accustomed place or set of association.
   Synonyms: alienate, disaffect.[18]

e*stranged*

1. Having become a stranger, of one who formerly was close, as a relative, friend, lover, or spouse.
   A semi-formal alternative definition is *not on speaking terms*.[19]

Someone can become estranged because of something as simple as an inadvertent misinterpretation of what someone else said. A variation of this occurs when someone speaks sooner than their mind can select the proper sequence of words to clarify their thought. What ends up being said is not what they were thinking. For example, someone might say, "You would be fortunate to have this person work for you." The intention might be to express that the prospective employee is a strong contributor to success. The prospective employer, however, might interpret this as an indication that it is difficult to get the person to perform their tasks. A fleeting distraction can cause a misinterpretation as well. It is not difficult to envision many other reasons.

If an angry response causes a shutdown in communication, an innocent error can go unresolved. John Townsend stresses the need for communication to facilitate a properly functioning family. He proposes that

---

[18]   *The Free Dictionary*, s.v. "estranged," accessed March 2013, http://www. thefreedictionary.com/estranged.html.

[19]   *Wiktionary, the free dictionary*, s.v. "Estranged," accessed March 2013, http:// en.wiktionary.org/wiki/estranged.html.

God has made the family an incubator in which our sense of basic trust and dependency is formed . . . But if our emotional needs are not . . . met . . . we will experience instead a feeling of aloneness and emptiness.

Safety in the family also means that: . . . family members reinforce vulnerability among themselves by taking the initiative to ask about each others' feelings.

Family members are emotionally warm and gentle when hurt feelings are expressed.[20]

Estrangement can also result from a misinterpretation of someone's intentions. A person may have experienced a particular situation in which their feelings were deeply hurt, or even worse, they may have been physically harmed. They might end up associating that result with any similar situation regardless of who the other person might be the next time around. In that case, they might assume the next individual will hurt them as well. However, the next person may be the nicest individual on earth and not understand why they are being shunned or rejected. The previously injured person might even lash out in self-defense. The good-natured individual would not know why. Two people who otherwise might have become best of friends end up in an estranged relationship.

To whatever degree, estrangement always seems to be associated with intimacy and related expectations. Positive expectations can go unsatisfied, or negative expectations can manifest due to a preconceived notion of futility. Either or both might manifest as a result of wishful thinking or an imagined condition that simply does not exist. Because intimacy entails transparency, the person becomes exposed and vulnerable. As mentioned, this is a necessary part

---

[20]   Dave Carder et al., *Unlocking Your Family Patterns* (Chicago, IL: Moody Publishers, 1991, 1993, 2011), 121, 122.

of life. Without it, every human would perish immediately upon exiting the womb. Although cultures may vary in their exact definition of what constitutes a family, no one escapes being vulnerable at birth. Therefore, each culture has some form of a life-sustaining process or system to nurture their offspring. Regardless of culture, it is the first moment of intimacy for each person on earth. It influences how that infant will respond to the next human contact, in whatever form of family any particular culture embraces.

If it can be agreed that no one is perfect, then it can be expected that every family harbors at least one member who is attempting to cover up some form of guilt or shame. If so, each child starts his or her journey exposed to a certain degree of dysfunctioning. However, the primal need for intimacy remains. A parent might withhold intimacy or correction if that action is going to somehow expose a guilt or shame the parent is hoping to keep secret. Intimacy is broken, and the child's need is not satisfied. As the child grows, it will seek the satisfaction elsewhere. Sometimes, the residue can extend well into adulthood, and the dysfunction carries into subsequent generations.

Chuck Swindoll mentions causes and consequences such as "incest, child molestation, brutality, addiction" and victims who "suffer in silence, feeling alienated and ashamed."[21]

Dave Carder presents a case study of Julie, who "suffered from an extreme lack of attention and love from her parents, and the harsh punishment served as a form of attention, however excessive and abusive, from her parents. An unwritten rule in a dysfunctional family is that it is better to be picked on than to be ignored."[22]

---

[21] Dave Carder et al., *Unlocking Your Family Patterns* (Chicago, IL: Moody Publishers, 1991, 1993, 2011), 7.

[22] Dave Carder et al., *Unlocking Your Family Patterns* (Chicago, IL: Moody Publishers, 1991, 1993, 2011), 12.

Barbara LeBey also offers vivid examples of reasons for, and consequences of, generational family dysfunctions:

> Messy divorce, an in-law problem, an interracial marriage, leaving a religion or joining another one, a family business that fails, conflict over an inheritance, an adult child's announcement that s/he is gay, one sibling taking on the sole burden of caring for aging parents . . .

> A son who shouts hurtful words in anger, a parent who's never there because s/he is a workaholic, a father who can't express his love, a mother who can't offer praise, a daughter who wants more than the family can afford and berates them for their lack of means. Parents are often hurt by children who take their love and generosity for granted. Parents hurt children by neglecting, abusing or shortchanging them. Siblings hurt each other by disloyalty, rivalry or abuse.

> A son loves his father but grows to hate the Dad after . . . the father remarries, has another family and loses touch with his son. A son loves the mother . . . but grows to hate her for not accepting his spouse. A daughter loves the mother . . . but hates her for being drunk most of the time.[23]

Additional causes and consequences are offered by Henry Cloud, including the following: "Dad's drinking problem . . . Derrick's behavior problems . . . Susan's depression and isolation . . . Derrick's inability to make friends."[24]

The National Institutes of Health adds the following causes and consequences: "The birth of a sibling, a divorce, or death in the family may

---

[23] Barbara LeBey, *Family Estrangements* (Atlanta, GA: Longstreet Press, 2001).

[24] Dave Carder et al., *Unlocking Your Family Patterns* (Chicago, IL: Moody Publishers, 1991, 1993, 2011), 161.

cause a child to act out . . . a pattern of hostile, aggressive, or disruptive behaviors . . . not appropriate for the child's age."[25]

What seems common to all estranged family situations is the connection back to the infancy stage of a child's development. Events later in life can exacerbate a dysfunction that began many years earlier.

It is not uncommon to observe how consequences associated with family estrangement can be paralyzing for many. Perhaps there is a correlation to the events that paralyze so many individuals and families in the Middle East. How does an infant's need for intimacy translate to the mounting tensions in that region? How does generational dysfunction translate to the tension? It is alarming that news media find no shortage of coverage to show these tensions spreading to many other places. Can the analysis of estranged family characteristics provide any clue to finding a remedy? Perhaps at the very least, struggling families will benefit from this exploration.

In his book *The Racial and Cultural Divide*, Dr. Cedrick D. Brown provides some insight. His observations from the Bible have corresponding verses in the Qur'an, which is very often the case. In the Qur'an, Surah 2:213 states, "Men belonged to a single community, and God sent them messengers to give them happy tidings and warnings." In a similar observation, Dr. Brown recognizes that universal intimacy was indeed present prior to Abraham. Cedrick Brown quotes, "Now the whole earth used the same language and the same words" (Genesis 11:1). Considering that Dr. Brown's observation finds substance in both the Qur'an and the Bible, there seem no grounds for estrangement at that point in history. Cedrick Brown goes on to say, "God's perfect plan was for mankind to live as one . . . But . . . the people . . . wanted to make a name for themselves . . . Today we still have the same tendency,

---

[25] US National Library of Medicine *NIH* National Institutes of Health, "MedlinePlus—Child Behavior Disorders," accessed September 2013, http://www.nim.nih.gov/medlineplus/childbehaviordisorders.html.

that is, to preserve 'my' race or 'my' culture . . . Please . . . I'm not advocating diminishing anyone's race and cultural identity."[26] In other words, it becomes dysfunctional to elevate race and/or culture above caring for others despite race or culture. The tendency noted by Dr. Brown is reflected in Surah 2:213: "God sent . . . the Book . . . but only those who received it differed . . . on account of . . . (jealousies) among them." The *Book* is the Islam term for the Bible. The Qur'an identifies the Israelites as those who received the Book and gives them the title *Children of the Book*. In other words, Surah 2:213 might imply that the Israelites were preserving a name for themselves and elevating culture above caring for others.

As established above, harmony remained intact at this point in history. A probable point of division is submitted later in this study. Meanwhile, it makes sense that the disharmony must relate to something common to the three major Abrahamic religions. What seems common among them is the regard for knowing right from wrong. It is also common to find members of all three faiths, at one time or another, thinking and acting contrary to what their respective faith commands. If no one is perfect, then it makes sense that this anomaly would be found in every person, regardless of faith (or lack thereof). Notwithstanding, one might expect that all descendants of Abraham should be making best efforts to do what God says to do, and refrain from what God says not to do. Anything contrary to these principles is what Abraham's God refers to as sin.[27] Bruno Giamba asserts that when someone sins, "we either can run toward God or run away, which leads to covering up."

J. Grathmore Stratus III has already documented how covering up can lead to estranged family situations. Ironically, Mr. Giamba asserts, "You don't

---

26   Cedrick Brown, *The Racial and Cultural Divide* (Mustang, OK: Tate, 2009).

27   M. H. Shakir, trans. Surahs 4:31; 12:97; 67:11; 69:9; 68:12, *Concordance of the Qur'an* (Elmhurst, NY: Tahrike Tarsile Qur'an, 2005); Isaiah 59:2; James 4:17, *New American Standard Bible*, bilingual ed. (Anaheim, CA: Foundation Publications, 1960).

need to hide from Him because you will miss out on the awesome blessing of being intimate with *Him*!!!" As previously shown, each person is born with the need for intimacy. The ultimate intimacy that God desires to share is willingly pushed away when a person attempts to cover up their wrongdoing before God. Bruno Giamba concludes that we do need to hide and cover the wrong, but that "God wants to be your hiding place! He wants to be your covering! You will receive grace, mercy, joy, peace and hope!!!"[28] Perhaps this irony contains a clue. At this point, the question becomes who and/or what is this god, the God of Abraham?

---

[28] Bruno R. Giamba, "Let's Get Real" (sermon, Souderton, Pennsylvania, August 2013).

CHAPTER THREE

ABRAHAM'S GOD

The intention here is not to convince anyone that God exists. The freedom to believe whatever one chooses is a cherished right and honored by this author. If a reader who does not believe in God can bear a momentary irritation, they too can gain valuable insight into the complexity inherent to estranged family situations. The reader will also gain insight into the media reports of turmoil and animosity from the Middle East. That volatility provides an excellent example of the estranged family situation and unnecessary generational harm.

Assume for a moment that there is no absolute truth. Is that absolutely true? If it is then there seems to be an inherent contradiction to the assumption. Either way, the freedom to believe whatever one chooses remains a cherished right. Apparently, the three Abrahamic religions choose to believe in an absolute truth. Each absolutely believes their spiritual roots trace back to Abraham.[29] In a more genetic sense, "Abrahamic religions are . . . faiths emphasizing and tracing their common origin to Abraham . . . all . . . claim a direct lineage to Abraham."[30] Despite their common roots, their relations have become

---

[29] F. E. Peters, *The Children of Abraham* (Princeton, NJ: Princeton University Press, 2004), 1.

[30] *Wikipedia, the free encyclopedia*, s.v. "Abrahamic religions," accessed April 2013, http://en.wikipedia/wiki/Abrahamic_religions.htm.

estranged. What happened, and where did the split occur? Was there more than one split? Perhaps the division is repeated generationally. Are the differences merely explained away by semantics? By way of example, in the same way that the Spanish word *Dios* translates to the English word *God*, the Arabic word *Allah* translates to the English word *God*. If God is God, then why is there an estranged situation existing within the family of Abraham's God? If not due to semantics, then perhaps the answer is related to faith and beliefs.

God promised a land to Abraham and his descendants, as recorded in Genesis 12:7 and 13:14-15 of the Bible. Islam's holy book is the Qur'an, and it refers to the Bible as "the Book." Muslim is the name given to followers of Islam. Muslim descendants are mostly of Arab origin. Most are members of the Islam faith whereby "Ibrahim (Abraham) is the first in a genealogy for Muhammad . . . the first monotheist in a world where monotheism was lost, and the community of those faithful to God . . . is descended from Abraham's son Ishmael. Muhammad, as an Arab, is descended from Abraham's son Ishmael."[31]

The faith of the Jewish descendants is Judaism, which "is considered by religious Jews to be the expression of the covenantal relationship God established with the Children of Israel. The Hebrews / Israelites were already referred to as 'Jew' in later books . . . such as the Book of Esther, with the term Jews replacing the title 'Children of Israel.'"[32] TheFreeDictionary.com defines *Hebrew* as "A member or descendant of a Semitic people claiming descent from Abraham, Isaac, and Jacob; an Israelite; a Jew . . . According to Jewish tradition, Abraham was the first post-Flood prophet to reject idiolatry . . .

---

[31] *Wikipedia, the free encyclopedia*, s.v. "Abrahamic religions," accessed April 2013, http://en.wikipedia/wiki/Abrahamic_religions.htm.

[32] *Wikipedia, the free encyclopedia*, s.v. "Judaism," accessed April 2013, http://en.wikipedia.org/wiki/Judaism.html.

although Shem and Eber carried on the tradition from Noah . . . Jews . . . are all identified as sons and daughters of Abraham and Sarah."[33]

In Christianity, "the emphasis is placed on faith being the only requirement for the Abrahmic Covenant to apply."[34] All three faiths trace their spiritual roots back to Abraham, "emphasizing . . . their common origin to Abraham or recognizing a spiritual tradition identified with him."[35] Among many others, Arabs and Jews can be traced back to the Semitic people who descended from Noah's son Shem. The word *Semitic* is derived from *Shem*, which appears in both Hebrew and Arabic languages.[36]

Academia defines *God* (capital *G*) as "often conceived as the supreme being and principal object of faith";[37] meanwhile defining *god* (lowercased *g*) as "a being or object believed to have more than natural attributes and powers and to require human worship; . . . a person or thing of supreme value . . . a powerful ruler."[38] It would seem that Abraham's children are divided based on a more intimate definition of God than they are based on academic definitions. Is there an impartial view that can objectively arbitrate and help each faction see correctly? Logic would seem to dictate that such objectivity requires an absolute truth.

---

[33]   *Wikipedia, the free encyclopedia*, s.v. "Abrahamic religions," accessed April 2013, http://en.wikipedia/wiki/Abrahamic_religions.htm.

[34]   *Wikipedia, the free encyclopedia*, s.v. "Abrahamic religions," accessed April 2013, http://en.wikipedia/wiki/Abrahamic_religions.htm.

[35]   *Wikipedia, the free encyclopedia*, s.v. "Abrahamic religions," accessed April 2013, http://en.wikipedia/wiki/Abrahamic_religions.htm.

[36]   *Wikipedia, the free encyclopedia*, s.v. "Semitic people," accessed April 2013, http://en.wikipedia.org/wiki/Semitic_people.html.

[37]   *Wikipedia, the free encyclopedia*, s.v. "God," accessed April 2013, http://en.wikipedia.org/wiki/God.html.

[38]   *Wikipedia, the free encyclopedia*, s.v. "God," accessed April 2013, http://en.wikipedia.org/wiki/God.html.

An interesting component of absolute truth was brought to the attention of J. Grathmore. While still in the research stage of this writing, the Boston Marathon bombing took place in April of 2013. A police officer acquaintance of this author mentioned the bombing and offered his profound statement: "What harm is it to believe in a higher power that leads to morality?" This officer did not appear to be interested in religion or desirous to force any particular belief. His voice inflection and body language seemed to reflect an impartial view, concerned more with a common-sense perspective. For the purpose of this study, assume for a moment that Abraham's God is the higher power to which this officer was referring. Moving forward, when this study utilizes the word *God* (capital *G*), it will refer to the God of Abraham. Based on this assumption, morality would be defined by God, regardless of how anyone might prefer their own definition. That said, why do the three major Abrahamic religions have different views on how the God of Abraham defines morality? Which definition of morality is the one that should operate in society?

God is clearly defined in both the Qur'an and the Bible. Reading either one, He is found to be eternal, the creator, self-sufficient, all-knowing, kindhearted, tender, giving, providential, compassionate, omnipresent, and the only fair and just final judge. A concordance for each book is listed in the bibliography found at the back of this study. One is listed for the Qur'an, and another is listed for the Bible. Each characteristic of God can be readily confirmed by the reader. But is God merely something to be confirmed? Assume for a moment that even those people who do not believe in a God are suddenly convinced that His existence has been confirmed. Is that all there is? What is it about this God that gives His existence any value? The lives of Abraham and his descendants reveal that God desires intimacy with His creation. It demonstrates that God is personally interested and moves in the lives of people. But why would a self-sufficient deity need intimacy with humans? The obvious answer is that He does not need it. Instead, God desires it, as reflected in both the Qur'an and the Bible. In the Qur'an, God reflects a degree of jealousy, desiring to be mankind's only god. Consider Surah 6:46, "'Imagine if God takes away your hearing and sight, and sets a seal on your hearts, what deity other than God will restore them to you?'" It appears that to remain mankind's only god, if necessary, God would remove sight and hearing to ensure mankind cannot be drawn away to any other. In the Bible, God specifically reveals He is jealous (Exodus 20:5). For that very reason, in Exodus 20:3, God instructs that mankind "have no other gods before Me." Abraham's record seems to reflect that God's desire for intimacy with His creation is motivated by love. Surah 20:41 records God saying, "I chose you for Myself" while in Isaiah 43:7 of the Bible, God says, "Everyone . . . I have created for My glory."

God desires a family in the same way Abraham desired a family, and in the same way, all mankind desires to have children. Human infants are born in the image of the parents. In a similar manner, the Qur'an reflects man as having attributes of God. Surahs 5:64 and 48:10 confirm that God has hands while Surah 25:59 establishes that God can sit and that He can also stand.[39] In other words, mankind's hands and the ability to sit and stand are made in God's image. In agreement, well-known Bible verses in Genesis chapter 2 state, "'Let Us make man in Our image'" (Gen. 2:26), and "God created man in His own image . . . male and female" (Gen. 2:27). Surahs 44:38-39 record God saying, "We have not created the heavens and the earth . . . out of play. We created them with definite purpose." Like any parent, God has established a home for His children. In Genesis 2:28, God instructed the male and female to "'be fruitful and multiply, and . . . rule over . . . the earth.'"

Arguably, God desires that His love be reciprocated. That is intimacy. It is reflected in Surah 50:16: "We created man and . . . We are closer to him than his jugular vein." God's desire for sharing among His children is reflected in Surah 67:15: "It is He who made the earth . . . that you may travel all around it, and eat of things He has provided." In the Bible, Genesis 2:18 records how God ensured continuity of family intimacy: "Then the LORD God said, 'It is

---

[39] M. H. Shakir, trans., *Concordance of The Qur'an* (Elmhurst, NY: Tahrike Tarsile Qur'an, 2005), 1089.

not good for the man to be alone; I will make him a helper suitable for him.'" A person reciprocates God's love back to Him when that person places the needs of others ahead of their own needs. This is defined in Surah 2:267: "Give in charity . . . of the things you have earned, and of what you produce from the earth; and do not choose to give what is bad as alms, that is, things you would not like to accept yourself." Surah 3:92 qualifies that a degree of pain is associated with the sacrifice made to care for others: "You will never come to piety unless you spend of things you love." The Bible instructs, "Do not say to your neighbor, 'Go, and come back, and tomorrow I will give it,' when you have it with you" (Proverbs 3:28). It would be difficult to imagine a situation where considering others as more important than self can be accomplished without a sacrifice that entails some degree of pain from losing something close, cherished, and personal.

In his book *The Children of Abraham*, F. E. Peters states, "Judaism, Christianity, and Islam were born . . . when . . . God appeared to . . . Abram and bound him in a covenant forever . . . The history of monotheism had begun. The Covenant was made with Abraham and its rewards were promised to his heirs . . . Jews claim the Covenant . . . by reason of both their linear descent from Abraham . . . and their fidelity to its terms. Christians . . . contend that . . . the promise had been redrawn as a New Covenant and they were its heirs through their faith . . . Muslims . . . claim the inheritance . . . by a return to the original 'religion of Abraham,'" via the revelation to Muhammad." Mr. Peters points out a truth known to all three faiths. Abraham "originated in what is today Iraq—'Ur of the Chaldees.'"[40] At that time, his name was Abram. Today, Iraq is an Arab state associated with the Muslim faith. This is a very important point and needs to be given the credit due. It seems to be a reasonable place to begin a study of how God planned to establish His family through Abraham. It is hoped that this study helps each reader find the truth to restoring harmony that once existed, regardless of belief, culture, or race. Hopefully, each reader

---

[40]   F. E. Peters, *The Children of Abraham* (Princeton, NJ: Princeton University Press, 2004), 1, 7, 21.

will come to realize that God retains His desire to restore harmony and will secure eternal peace for His family.

Background information for this investigation is challenged on a daily basis. It should be realized that the Qur'an (Islam) was revealed (AD 611-632),[41] almost six hundred years after the New Testament (Christian) was recorded (AD 55-65.).[42] The New Testament picks up some four hundred years or so after the last book in the Old Testament (Hebrew) (Malachi, ca. 430 BC).[43] Tracing back to Abraham[44] adds another 1,660 years for a total gap of approximately 2,700 years. As Mr. Peters points out, however, Islam maintains that the Qur'an's revelator, "Muhammed enjoyed an absolute originality, remote from either texts or informants, and was in communication with God alone . . . But even if we grant that the Prophet delivered the Quran without any assistance from teachers or other people's books or stories . . . How could his audience in early seventh-century Mecca have possibly understood the Quran's . . . references to Abraham, Moses, Jesus, and the other prophets without some familiarity . . . with biblical material and related apocrypha?"[45] In other words, during the 2,700 years prior to Islam, the pre-Muslim people must have had some way of preserving the instructions God imparted to Abraham in order to guide their faith in God. This study has searched to find such a method and record without success. What has been found are variations of the position that, "Muslims view the Bible as having been changed and corrupted by Jews and

---

[41]   R. Ghattas and C. Ghattas, *A Christian Guide to the Qur'an* (Grand Rapids, MI: Kregel, 2009), 13.

[42]   *Life Application Study Bible* (Wheaton, IL: Tyndale House Publishers, 1991), 1722.

[43]   W. Elwell and R. Yarbrough, *Encountering the New Testament*, 2nd ed. (Grand Rapids, MI: Baker, 1998), 22.

[44]   "Bible Timeline," http://bibletimeline.info/.

[45]   F. E. Peters, *The Children of Abraham* (Princeton, NJ: Princeton University Press, 2004), 32, 33.

Christians."[46] Presumably, the pre-Muslim people were guided by the Bible, excepting the points they believe were altered by Jewish scribes. Surah 2:87 states, "Remember We gave Moses the Book . . . and to Jesus, son of Mary, We gave . . . truth" while Surah 3:79 reads, "Become learned . . . by virtue of teaching and studying the Book (Islam's name for the Bible)." Surah 40:53 confirms, "Verily We bequeathed the Book to the children of Israel." Although recorded thousands of years later than the Book (the Bible), the Qur'an appears accurate in naming the participants before and after Abraham. For example, Surah 21, verses 83-84 and 87-88, reads, "[Remember] Job when he called to his Lord . . . So We heard his cry and . . . we restored his family to him, . . . and gave him . . . grace from Us . . . And [remember] Dhu 'n-Noon [Jonah of the fish], . . . he called out from the darkness: 'surely I was a sinner' . . . We heard his cry, and saved him from anguish. That is how We deliver those who believe."

Surah 21 then speaks of the virgin birth in verse 91: "[Remember] her who preserved her chastity, into whom We breathed a new life from Us, and made her and her son a token for mankind." The New Testament speaks of the virgin's child as being conceived of the Holy Spirit. The Holy Spirit has been described and associated with breath, breeze and wind (Matthew 3:16; Luke 1:35; Acts 2:1-4). In the *Concordance of The Qur'an*, Surah 16:102 is translated as "The Holy Spirit has revealed." With all due respect, this study recognizes the caveat in Surahs 13:37 and 42:7, which assert that the Qur'an was revealed in Arabic to preserve understanding. However, hope of understanding to non-Arabic speaking people is found in Surah 17:45-46. This associated Surah elaborates, "When you recite the Qur'an, We place a hidden veil between you and those who do not believe in the Hereafter . . . that they should not understand it." In other words, there are many Jews and Christians who do believe in the hereafter. By default, they would not be precluded from

---

[46]   F. E. Peters, *The Children of Abraham* (Princeton, NJ: Princeton University Press, 2004), 3; *Wikipedia, the free encyclopedia*, s.v. "Abrahamic religions," accessed April 2013, http://en.wikipedia/wiki/Abrahamic_religions.htm.

the ability to understand the Qur'an. This adds to the hope for reconciliation in the estranged family of Abraham's God. It seems worth the while to continue with this study.

The details and chronology of Abraham's life, as well as that of his descendants, seem easier to follow in the Bible. This is not an implication of deficiency or inferiority in product. It is suggested merely because of format. Hopefully, Islam readers will look past anything considered as skewed in the text and permit use of the biblical account to help with the mapping sequence. Best efforts will be made to identify the points of difference, according to the research and references listed in this study's bibliography. No offense is intended, and each reader is encouraged to form his or her own conclusions.

According to chapter 11 in Genesis, Abram descended from Noah's son Shem as follows: Shem, Arpachshad, Shelah, Eber, Peleg, Rue, Serug, Nahor, and finally, Terah, who fathered Abram and his brothers Nahor and Haran. Haran fathered Lot and subsequently "died . . . in the land of his birth, in Ur of the Chaldeans" (Genesis 11:28). Other than the instruction to enter the land of Canaan, it is unclear why Terah departed as recorded in Genesis 11:31. He brought with him Lot, Abram, and Abram's barren wife, Sarai. They settled in Haran, which is some nine hundred miles or so to the north-northeast of Ur. It appears they opted to go around the desert that lies between Ur and Canaan. Traveling this route kept them close to the life-sustaining Euphrates River. Terah died in Haran, so in Genesis 12:1-2, "the LORD said to Abram 'Go forth . . . to the land which I will show you.'" To no surprise, that land is identified as Canaan in Genesis 12:5. Genesis 12:5-6 records that Abram passed into the land occupied by the Canaanite and brought Sarai and Lot to Shechem. The route traversed approximately 550 miles and appears to follow rivers.[47] From a standpoint of survival, this makes sense. It may have been the overall route Terah had in mind to begin with, when they departed Ur. In

---

[47] *New American Standard Bible*, bilingual ed. (Anaheim, CA: Foundation Publications, 1960), Maps 1, 2.

Genesis 12:7, "The LORD appeared to Abram and said, 'To your descendants, I will give this land.'" The word *descendant* in the original Hebrew used for this verse is "seed of the patriarchs [esp. Abr.]."[48] Considering both Islam and Judeo-Christian followers consider themselves descendants of Abram, it would seem there should be no disharmony between them up to this further point in history.

As a result of famine, Abram journeyed into Egypt, and eventually he departed from there. In the Bible, Genesis 13:3 records that the family eventually resided between Bethel and Ai, "where his tent had been at the beginning." This location is found in what is now modern-day Israel, just to the north of Jerusalem. The three communities of Sechem, Bethel, and Ai all reside close to each other.[49] Genesis 13:7 records that, "The Canaanite and the Perizzite were dwelling then in the land." Considering that neither the Jewish nor Islam faiths had been formalized at this point, the Canaanites and Perizzites were not worshippers of Abraham's God. Subsequent verses up through Genesis 13:12 depict how an estrangement was averted when strife arose between the herdsmen of Abram and those of Lot. Abram settled in Canaan while Lot chose to journey eastward "as far as Sodom." They agreed to this as "brothers" (Gen. 13:8). To the east would have taken Lot around the top of the Dead Sea, down the eastern side to near the bottom. That is the suspected location of Sodom. The area seems to border what became Edom, at Edom's northern part.[50] Genesis 13:14-15 states that "the LORD said to Abram, after Lot had separated from him . . . look . . . northward and southward and eastward and westward; for all the land which you see, I will give it

---

48   Jay P. Green Sr., *The Interlinear Bible,* Hebrew-Greek-English, 2nd ed. (Peabody, MA: Hendrickson, 1986), 9; Francis Brown et al., *Hebrew and English Lexicon* (Peabody, MA: Hendrickson, 2001), 282.

49   *New American Standard Bible*, bilingual ed. (Anaheim, CA: Foundation Publications, 1960), Maps 2, 10.

50   *New American Standard Bible*, bilingual ed. (Anaheim, CA: Foundation Publications, 1960), Maps 1, 2.

to . . . your descendants forever." The Hebrew word used here for *descendants* is the same as was used previously. It means "seed of the patriarchs [esp. Abr.].[51]" Once again, it seems that up to this point in history, there should be no disharmony, no dysfunction, and no estrangement. It is not dysfunctional for family members to move away from one another. This is what happens when two people marry and become one. However, as established in chapter 2, dysfunction occurs when the separation is due to misunderstanding, anger, or hurt feelings.

Identification of Abram's descendants appears in Genesis chapter 15. In verse 4, God tells Abram, "One who will come forth from your own body, he shall be your heir." God did not speak in terms of multiple children from Abram's body; He merely stated one. If multiple children were to come from Abram's body, God did not say which one would be the heir. Customary treatment of inheritance in either Jewish or Islamic tradition cannot be relied on here to determine the order of inheritance. The two religions did not yet exist. No custom or tradition had developed yet. This seems to indicate a crucial revelation, which can easily be overlooked. It appears that God's promise and inheritance are not based on custom, tradition, or religion. What then, is the binding element? Genesis 15:6 elaborates that Abram "believed in the LORD; and He reckoned it to him as righteousness." Could this be why God audibly spoke to Abraham, but no longer speaks audibly now? What does the intangible phrase "reckoned to him as righteousness" really mean? The more tangible elements can be readily researched. For example, the original word for *heir* in Genesis 15:4 means "succeeding to; taking the place of others, take possession of." The word for *believe* means "trust, and standing firm in it" while the word for *righteousness* means "ethically right, associated with justice

---

[51]   Jay P. Green Sr., *The Interlinear Bible,* Hebrew-Greek-English, 2nd ed. (Peabody, MA: Hendrickson, 1986), 9; Francis Brown et al., *Hebrew and English Lexicon* (Peabody, MA: Hendrickson, 2001), 282.

and virtue."[52] The Qur'an and the Bible confirm God is the only righteous one, the only perfect one; yet God considers Abraham righteous. Is the tangible land the object of inheritance, or is the object of inheritance something intangible? Perhaps righteousness is the object of inheritance. Better yet, perhaps the method to attain righteousness is what God had in mind. If so, what is that method that is supposed to be inherited? There were no Islamic or Judeo customs of traditions existing to define the method. Perhaps the method can be found as this study continues.

In summary to this point, God is looking for intimacy with mankind, as demonstrated in the relationship between God and Abraham. A two-part question evolves here: do all three Abrahamic religions trust the same God, and how and/or why does trust in that God translate into righteousness? In other words, how does imperfection pass into the realm that requires perfection? Both the Qur'an and the Bible speak of the necessity for perfection in order to reside with God in paradise. "Can a blind man and one who can see be equal? Or can darkness and light be the same?" That is the illustration provided in Surah 13:16. The earlier Surah regarding Jonah equated darkness with sin. The Bible also illustrates a distinct separation of imperfection from perfection in Genesis 16:7-8, 13: "Now the angel of the LORD found . . . Hagar . . . Then she called the name of the LORD . . . 'Have I even remained alive here after seeing Him?'" In other words, Hagar's rhetorical statement recognizes that her imperfection in the presence of the Lord should have destroyed her because imperfection can not reside with perfection. Was her belief, her faith, reckoned to her as righteousness? After all, the precedent was already set with Abraham. Maybe Hagar was placing her trust in—and basing her life upon—the God who made the promise, rather than basing her life on the promise itself? Once again, the reader is free to decide.

[52] Jay P. Green Sr., *The Interlinear Bible,* Hebrew-Greek-English, 2nd ed. (Peabody, MA: Hendrickson, 1986); Francis Brown et al., *Hebrew and English Lexicon* (Peabody, MA: Hendrickson, 2001), 282.

CHAPTER FOUR

ABRAHAM'S FIRST CHILD

The record of Abraham picks up in chapter 16 of Genesis, starting in verse 1: "Now Sarai, Abram's wife had borne him no children and she had an Egyptian maid whose name was Hagar. So Sarai said to Abram . . . 'Please go in to my maid; perhaps I will obtain children through her' . . . Sarai took Hagar . . . and gave her to her husband Abram as his wife" (Gen. 16:1-3). The original word *wife* as used for Sarai is the same word used for Hagar.[53] The word *concubine* was not used to identify Hagar. This seems to present an illustration that God is not necessarily concerned with semantics. God's number one concern is people. God was intimately and equally concerned with both Hagar and Sarai. Continuing with Genesis 16:4, 6, 11, 12, "When she saw that she had conceived, her mistress was despised in her sight . . . So Sarai treated her harshly, and she fled . . . The angel of the LORD said to her ' . . . you are with child, . . . And you shall call his name Ishmael . . . and he will live to the east of all his brothers.'" The original Hebrew word used for *son* in

---

[53]   Jay P. Green Sr., *The Interlinear Bible,* Hebrew-Greek-English, 2nd ed. (Peabody, MA: Hendrickson, 1986), 9; Francis Brown et al., *Hebrew and English Lexicon* (Peabody, MA: Hendrickson, 2001), 282.

this instance means "a male child, born of a woman, a son (as a builder of the family name)."[54]

To eventually live east of his brothers, Ishmael would have most likely followed a route similar to the route taken by Lot when he left Abram. While still in his teens, Ishmael's departure came at the request of his Aunt Sarai. In Genesis 17:4-5, 7-8, God told Abram, "My covenant is with you, And you will be the father of a multitude of nations . . . your name shall be Abraham . . . I will establish . . . between Me and you and your descendants . . . throughout their generations for an everlasting covenant . . . to you and to your descendants . . . the land of Canaan for an everlasting possession." Albeit everlasting, it would appear the land was associated more with possession than with the covenant. The word *covenant* here is a binding agreement between God and man requiring loyalty and obedience.[55]

The record resumes in Genesis 17:15, 19-21, where God instructs Abraham, "'As for Sarai . . . Sarah shall be her name . . . Sarah . . . will bear you a son, and you shall call his name Isaac, and I will establish My covenant with him for an everlasting covenant for his descendants after him. As for Ishmael . . . I will bless him . . . he shall become the father of twelve princes and I will make him a great nation . . . But my covenant I will establish with Isaac.'" In the Qur'an, Surah 44:30 reads, "So We saved the children of Israel . . . And We exalted them over the other people" (verse 32). Surah 44:37 qualifies this rhetorically: "Are they better than the people . . . whom We destroyed as . . . sinners?" It is important to look at what was originally contemplated in regard

---

[54] Jay P. Green Sr., *The Interlinear Bible,* Hebrew-Greek-English, 2nd ed. (Peabody, MA: Hendrickson, 1986); Francis Brown et al., *Hebrew and English Lexicon* (Peabody, MA: Hendrickson, 2001).

[55] Jay P. Green Sr., *The Interlinear Bible*, Hebrew-Greek-English; 2nd ed. (Peabody, MA: Hendrickson, 1986); Francis Brown et al., *Hebrew and English Lexicon* (Peabody, MA: Hendrickson, 2001); James Strong, *Strong's Exhaustive Concordance of the Bible* (Peabody, MA: Hendrickson [undated]).

to the word *possession* as used in Genesis 17:8. The original word simply means "land possessed . . . by right of inheritance."[56] God did not say that the covenant with Isaac is to replace any other covenant. There remains a covenant applicable to all Abraham's descendants, and it seems to be faith oriented more than material oriented, as already mentioned. The faith-oriented view lends itself more toward preserving family function while a material-oriented view has the potential to spark estrangements in the family. Either way, it appears that God intimately and equally loved both Ishmael and Isaac.

In Genesis 21:10, Sarah insists that Abraham "'drive out this maid and her son, for the son of this maid shall not be an heir with my son Isaac.'" This reaction seems to reflect jealousy, envy, possessiveness, and loathing that caused dysfunction in the family. It clearly indicates estrangement. Genesis 21:14 records that Hagar and Ishmael "wandered about in the wilderness of Beersheba." Ishmael living in the east would obviously come later. Meantime, in Genesis 21:13, God reiterates that Ishmael is a descendant of Abraham, and it comes subsequent to the mention of covenant in specific context to Isaac. However, the same original Hebrew word for *descendant* is used in respect of both Ishmael and Isaac. Rather than continue in context associating with Isaac's name, it is interesting that God subsequently brings the giving of land back in context with the word *descendants*. Perhaps land is not what God ultimately had in mind when He spoke in terms of covenant. Perhaps it had more to do with attempts to cover up sin. From what was learned earlier, it seems that Sarah was attempting to remove the reminder of her guilt by having Hagar and Ishmael displaced. In Genesis 16:5, she confesses that it was wrong to have given her handmaid to Abram and wrong for Abram to have expedited the idea. "And Sarai said to Abram, 'May the LORD judge between you and me.'" Abram gave in to the pressure rather than execute his responsibility. It is reminiscent of Adam's failure to take the lead when he and his wife were faced

---

[56] Jay P. Green Sr., *The Interlinear Bible,* Hebrew-Greek-English, 2nd ed. (Peabody, MA: Hendrickson, 1986); Francis Brown et al., *Hebrew and English Lexicon* (Peabody, MA: Hendrickson, 2001).

with temptation. Adam gave in to the pressure as well. Both Adam and Abram should have known better. The cover-up for Adam and Eve was leaves. The cover-up for Abram and Sarai was the expulsion of two family members from the home. Both events are good illustrations of estranged-family subject matter. Adam and Eve had a secret. Perhaps there was a moment when their son Cain required correcting but did not happen because it might have required them to expose their secret. What if it would have been the correction that kept his character righteous? What if that, in turn, prevented Cain from murdering his brother Abel? Would a covenant based on tangible items such as land prevent such tragedy? Perhaps it would, but it seems more likely that a covenant based on a method to attain righteousness would be a more effective prevention. The author merely presents these thoughts for consideration.

If readers remain open to the idea that a method to righteousness might be the object of covenant, then this study continues for their further consideration. Obviously, the method God had in mind predates the customs, traditions, and beliefs of religious systems that simply did not yet exist at that time. God was and remains interested in reconciliation and intimacy, regardless of lineage. Murder is a wrongdoing that requires reconciliation with God. God remained intimate even in the midst of such a horrific sin. "'Where is Abel your brother?' the LORD inquired" (Genesis 4:9). Cain replied, "Am I my brother's keeper?" God demonstrates here that His intention for all mankind is to care for one another. If the land is an inheritance to all Abraham's descendants, both Muslims and Jews have a right to usage. In Surah 14:48, the Qur'an speaks of the earth being replaced. Surah 55:26-27 states, "All that is on the earth is passing, But abiding is the glory of your Lord" while the Bible says, "The grass withers, the flower fades, But the word of our God stands forever" (Isaiah 40:8). The covenant refers to something that is everlasting. It does not seem to make sense that the covenant would be referring to land, because land withers and is not everlasting. Insisting that land is the object of covenant might serve to perpetuate the estrangement that exists in the family of Abraham's God. Tragic consequences continue to manifest in the Middle East and elsewhere.

Consider now the rhetorical question asked in Surah 2:211, "Ask the children of Israel . . . if one changes the favor of God after having received it [the Bible message], then remember, God is severe in revenge . . . . My word shall not be changed, nor am I in the least unjust" is the proclamation found in Surah 50:29. This corresponds to the warning in the Bible that God's word is not to be added to, changed, or have anything removed from it (Deuteronomy 4:2, 12:32; Psalms 89:34; John 14:26, 15:15; Galatians 1:8; Hebrews 13:8). It appears that something in God's instructions to mankind must have been changed somewhere at sometime to perpetuate the ongoing argument over land. Defining the two sides of this contention is necessary to understand the situation.

Surah 22:78 states, "Your forbear Abraham . . . He named you Muslim." This study is not in position to address this point, but as a courtesy to readers, it has been mentioned. Benefit of the doubt is given that Islam scholars will explain how there seems no record of Abraham practicing in the ways of Islam some 2,700 years before the Muslim faith and practice was established. Nevertheless, according to the Muslim faith, the transfer of God's promise descends through Ishmael.[57] "Muslims . . . claim the inheritance . . . by a return to the pristine form of monotheism, the 'religion of Abraham.'"[58] "An adherent of Islam is called a Muslim." "Muslims believe . . . scriptures . . . had become distorted . . . . The Qur'an is viewed . . . as the final revelation and literal word of God . . . *Allah* is the term with no plural or gender used by Muslims . . . to reference God while *'ilah* is the term used for a deity or a god in general."[59] This study is unable to explain how the Qur'an is viewed as the final revelation and literal word of God because in Surah 29:27, "God tells Muhammad that

---

[57]   *Wikipedia, the free encyclopedia*, s.v. "Ishmael," accessed September 2013, http:// en.wikipedia.org/wiki/Ishmael.

[58]   F. E. Peters, *The Children of Abraham* (Princeton, NJ: Princeton University Press, 2004), 21.

[59]   *Wikipedia, the free encyclopedia*, s.v. "Islam," accessed April 2013, http:// en.wikipedia.org/wiki/Islam.html.

He gave only Abraham, Isaac, Jacob, and their offspring the prophecy and the books.[60]" Here again, benefit of the doubt is given that Islam scholars have the explanation. Just because this study was unable to find their explanation does not mean that their explanation does not exist.

The word *Muslim* (also spelled Moslem) means "one who submits to God."[61] Similar to non-Messianic Jews, Muslims do not agree with the Christian Trinity of one God existing in three persons and character. They do, however, believe God provided Moses with the Torah, David with the Psalms, and Jesus with the Gospel. Most Arabs are Muslim; however, the title *Arab* predates the establishment of Islam, as mentioned in chapter 3. During the Assyrian conquest of Syria in ninth century BC, the first documented use of the term *Arab* was found in the Akkadian language.[62] "The Arab League . . . defines an Arab as . . . 'a person whose language is Arabic, who lives in an Arabic-speaking country, and who is in sympathy with the aspirations of the Arabic-speaking peoples.[63]'" Many Arab sects exist, but common to each is the origin of the Semitic language. "Most people who consider themselves Arab do so on the overlap of the political and linguistic definitions . . . . The Arabs are defined by their culture, not by race; and their culture is defined by . . . Arabism and Islam . . . Beyond that, he or she might be of any ancestry, of any religion or philosophical persuasion, and a citizen of any country . . . Being Arab does not contradict . . . being non-Muslim . . ." However, "The Qur'an does not use the word Arab . . . The Qur'an calls itself Arabic" (Surah 43:2-3). According to medieval Arab genealogists, "Arabized Arabs" include

---

[60]   R. Ghattas and C. Ghattas, *A Christian Guide to the Qur'an* (Grand Rapids, MI: Kregel, 2009).

[61]   *Wikipedia, the free encyclopedia*, s.v. "Muslim," accessed April 2013, http://en.wikipedia.org/wiki/Muslim.html.

[62]   *Wikipedia, the free encyclopedia*, s.v. "Muslim," accessed April 2013, http://en.wikipedia.org/wiki/Muslim.html.

[63]   *Wikipedia, the free encyclopedia*, s.v. "Arab," accessed April 2013, http://en.wikipedia.org/wiki/Arab.html.

"sons of Ishmael intermingled with the six sons of Keturah (a concubine of Abraham) . . . and their descendants were all called Arabs and Ishmaelites."[64] In terms of genealogy, ancestry is traced back to the original tribes of the Arabian Peninsula and Syrian Desert. It is not unreasonable to think that Ishmael, Lot, and their descendants helped propagate these areas. Ishmael, in particular, may have felt rejected, abandoned, and hurt, possibly leading to generational estrangement.

Lot was already separated from Abraham when Ishmael was expelled from Abraham's family. However, it is not likely that Lot would have felt as estranged as Ishmael may have felt. Ishmael was at least thirteen years old at the time he was forced to leave (Genesis 18:25). This part of the study reengages with Lot's life in Genesis 19. After God destroyed the wicked cities of Sodom and Gomorrah (Genesis 19:24-25), Lot's wife was lost during their escape (Genesis 19:26). His daughters assumed that Lot was the only male remaining on earth (Genesis 19:31). The daughters "made their father drink wine . . . and the firstborn went in . . . and he did not know when she lay down or when she arose" (Genesis 19:33). The process was repeated the following day with the younger daughter. "The firstborn bore a son, and called his name Moab; he is the father of the Moabites . . . the younger also bore a son, and . . . he is the father of the sons of Ammon" (Genesis 19:37-38).

Moabites and Ammonites are included the category of Semitic-speaking people. The word *Semite* comes from the name *Shem*, one of Noah's sons. It encompasses "Akkadinas (Assyrians and Babylonians), Eblaites, Ugarites, Canaanites, Phoenicians (including Carthaginians), Hebrews (Israelites, Judeans and Samaritans), Ahlamu, Arameans, Chaldeans, Amorites, Moabites, Edomites, Hykosos, Ishmaelites, Nabateans, Maganites, Shebans,

---

[64]   *Wikipedia, the free encyclopedia*, s.v. "Arab," accessed 2013, http://en.wikipedia. org/wiki/Arab.html; s.v. "Islam," accessed 2013, http://en.wikipedia.org/wiki/ Islam.html; s.v. "Abrahamic Religions," accessed 2013, http://en.wikipedia/wiki/ Abrahamic_religions.htm.

Sutu, Ubaries, Dilmunite, Bahranis, Maltese, Mandaeans, Sabians, Syriacs, Mhallami, Amalekites, Arabs, Palmyrans, and Qedarites." In addition to language, Semites are also "associated by close geographic . . . distribution."[65] Although originating from the Arabian Peninsula, Semitic people were obviously not Arabic speakers but did mix with non-Semitic people. They eventually "lost their political domination . . . due to internal turmoil and attacks by non-Semitic peoples."[66] Apparently, family dysfunction (internal turmoil) contributed to their ruin. Present-day Arabia is also referred to as the Arabian Peninsula and includes Saudi Arabia, Yemen, Oman, Bahrain, Qatar, Kuwait, and the United Arab Emirates (UAE).[67] It would not be difficult to imagine that offspring of both Lot and Ishmael intermixed in these regions.

As can best be discerned from biblical record, Ishmael was indeed Abraham's first child and obviously his firstborn son. Considering his forced departure, as intimated earlier, it is reasonable to expect that Ishmael may have felt rejected and/or abandoned. If Ishmael felt rejected, his nephew Esau may have shared a generational estrangement from feeling jilted and deceived. This study continues in Genesis 25:20-21, 23: "And Isaac . . . took . . . the daughter of . . . the Aramean . . . the sister of Laban the Aramean, to be his wife . . . and . . . his wife conceived . . . The Lord said to her, 'Two nations are in your womb; . . . And the older shall serve the younger." This presents another point of contention for the estranged family of Abraham's God. The word used here for *serve* means "enslaved."[68] In contrast to the traditional practice, the firstborn

---

[65] *Wikipedia, the free encyclopedia*, s.v. "Semitic people," accessed April 2013, http://en.wikipedia.org/wiki/Semitic_people.html.

[66] *Wikipedia, the free encyclopedia*, s.v. "Semitic people," accessed April 2013, http://en.wikipedia.org/wiki/Semitic_people.html.

[67] *The Free Dictionary*, s.v. "Arabia," accessed March 2013, http://www. thefreedictionary.com/Arabia.html.

[68] Jay P. Green Sr., *The Interlinear Bible*, Hebrew-Greek-English; 2nd ed. (Peabody, MA: Hendrickson, 1986); Francis Brown et al., *Hebrew and English Lexicon* (Peabody, MA: Hendrickson, 2001).

son taking a secondary role to the younger brother is found in two successive generations. The biblical record shows Isaac assuming the household position of first son despite being born after Ishmael. This also occurred with Jacob's sons. "Now the first came forth red . . . like a hairy garment; and they named him Esau. Afterward his brother came forth with his hand holding on to Esau's heel, so his name was called Jacob" (Gen. 25:25-26). Subsequently, as young men, in return for food, Esau sold his birthright to Jacob (Gen. 25:33). *Birthright* here means "the right of the firstborn."[69]

In Genesis 27, Isaac's wife Rebekah conspired with her son Jacob to deceive his father Isaac into giving Esau's blessing to Jacob. It was successful. The word *blessing* used here means "the blessing of a parent."[70] "May peoples serve you . . . Be master of your brothers, and may your mother's sons bow down to you" are some of the key ingredients of Isaac's blessing to Jacob (Gen. 27:29). "When Esau heard . . . he cried out with an exceedingly great and bitter cry . . . Jacob . . . took away my birthright, and . . . he has taken away my blessing" (Gen. 27:34, 36). In Genesis 27:39-41, "Isaac . . . said to him, 'Behold, away from the fertility of the earth shall be your dwelling . . . By your sword you shall live, And your brother you shall serve; but it shall come about when you become restless, that you will break his yoke from your neck' . . . So Esau bore a grudge against Jacob . . . and . . . said to himself . . . 'I will kill my brother Jacob.'"

Isaac's first son, Esau, "went to Ishmael [Isaac's brother] and married . . . the daughter of Ishmael" (Genesis 28:9). Later, in fear of encountering Esau, Jacob sent gifts ahead with the message that they come from "your servant

[69] Jay P. Green Sr., *The Interlinear Bible*, Hebrew-Greek-English; 2nd ed. (Peabody, MA: Hendrickson, 1986); Francis Brown et al., *Hebrew and English Lexicon* (Peabody, MA: Hendrickson, 2001).

[70] Jay P. Green Sr., *The Interlinear Bible*, Hebrew-Greek-English; 2nd ed. (Peabody, MA: Hendrickson, 1986); Francis Brown et al., *Hebrew and English Lexicon* (Peabody, MA: Hendrickson, 2001).

Jacob; it is a present to my lord Esau" (Genesis 32:18). As Esau approached, Jacob proceeded forward and stopped seven times to bow to the ground. "Then Esau ran to meet him and embraced him, and fell on his neck and kissed him, and they wept" (Genesis 33:1-4). This demonstration seems to indicate that humility is a necessary ingredient to reconciliation, and someone must take the first step by conceding.

Subsequently, Esau continued on to Seir (Genesis 33:14), which is toward the Gulf of Aqaba. According to Genesis 36:8, "Esau lived in the hill country of Seir; Esau is Edom." The land of Seir was inhabited by the Horites (Genesis 36:30). "Esau . . . killed off the Horites and took over the land . . . just as Israel did to the land of their possession."[71] The Bible records that the dispossession of the inhabitants was executed in accordance with instructions from God. This study has been unable to find record of a similar instruction to Esau regarding the Horites. This author is not in position to confirm whether or not such a record exists. Nonetheless, when Edom's prince allied with the Midian nation, Edom became an enemy of Solomon, the Hebrew king. Other points of interest include that Edom was referred to as Kushu by the Egyptians and that Mt. Seir is important for the purpose of locating Mt. Sinai.[72]

Before moving on from Abraham's first son, Ishmael, information found in research may be worth considering. If the source of the following information has been reported correctly, this information can provide valuable insight into the current hostilities existing in the estranged family of Abraham's God. "The Mahdi is Islam's Messiah, or Savior . . . University of Virginia Professor Abdulaziz Abdulhussein Sachedina . . . elaborates . . . 'The Islamic messiah . . . embodies . . . restoration of the purity of the Faith . . . creating . . . a world free from oppression" while "Sheikh Kabbani likewise identifies . . . Muslims are

---

[71] Steve Rudd, "The Edomites," http://www.bible.ca/archeology/bible-archeology-edomite-territory-mt-seir.htm.

[72] Steve Rudd, "The Edomites," http://www.bible.ca/archeology/bible-archeology-edomite-territory-mt-seir.htm.

waiting for both the Mahdi and Jesus." "Tradition . . . states that the Mahdi will descend from the family of Muhammad and will bear Muhammad's name . . . there is one particular hadith (Qur'an commentary) that places this event at the time of a final peace agreement between the Arabs and the Romans (referring to . . . the West) . . . for a period of seven years." According to Shaykh Muhammad Hisham Kabbini, chairman of the Islamic Supreme Council of America: "The coming of the Mahdi is established doctrine for both Sunni and Shi'a Muslims and indeed for all humanity." According to "a very famous tradition . . . throughout the Islamic world . . . 'The last hour would not come unless the Muslims will fight against the Jews and the Muslims would kill them.'"[73] If this information is true, then contention over land might not be the true issue underlying the hostilities in the Middle East. If Israel were to concede all land to the Arab nations, would the Mahdi waive the need to fight against and kill the Jews? Would the estrangement in the family cease? Would mankind's imperfection be covered with the perfection required for entrance into eternal paradise?

---

[73]   "The Mahdi: Islam's Awaited Messiah," accessed August 2013, http://www. answering-islam.org/Authors/JR/Future/ch04_the_mahdi.htm.

CHAPTER FIVE

COMPETITION ARRIVES

Competition for Abraham's inheritance unfolds in Genesis 17:19: "Sarah . . . will bear you a son, and you shall call his name Isaac." This is significant because Genesis 15:2 and 16:1 reveal that Sarah was unable to bear children. Moreover, it was considered impossible for a woman her age to bear a child, as expressed by Abraham in Genesis 17:17: "Will a child be born to a man one hundred years old? And will Sarah, who is ninety years old, bear a child?" This event feeds into a documented point of contention between faiths that exists in Genesis 22:1-3, 5, 10-12: "Now it came about . . . that God tested Abraham, and said . . . 'Take now your only son . . . Isaac, and go . . . offer him . . . as a burnt offering' . . . So Abraham . . . took two . . . young men . . . and Isaac . . . and he split wood for the burnt offering . . . and went . . . Abraham said to his young men, 'Stay here . . . and I and the lad will go . . . and return to you' . . . Abraham stretched out his hand and took the knife to slay his son . . . But the angel of the LORD called to him . . . 'Do . . . nothing to him, for now I know that you fear God.'"

"Islam holds that it was Ishmael . . . rather than Isaac, whom Ibrahim was instructed to sacrifice."[74] In speaking of Abraham, Surah 37, verses 100,

---

[74] *Wikipedia, the free encyclopedia*, s.v. "Abrahamic religions," accessed April 2013, http://en.wikipedia/wiki/Abrahamic_religions.htm.

103-107, and 111-112, record, "he prayed, 'Oh Lord, grant me a righteous son.' So We gave him the good news of a clement son . . . 'O my son, I dreamt that I was sacrificing you' . . . and [Abraham] laid [his son] down prostrate on his temple . . . We called out: 'O Abraham, You have fulfilled your dream' Thus . . . We reward the good . . . So we ransomed him . . . He is truly among Our faithful creatures. So We gave him the good news of Isaac . . . And we blessed him and Isaac." The author is unable to explain the contention because in Ahmed Ali's side-by-side Arabic English version of the Qur'an, Isaac is named and not Ishmael. This would seem to make sense considering Ishmael had departed to the wilderness, leaving Isaac as the son at home with Abraham. The Hebrew word used to describe Isaac is translated as *solitary*.[75] This might explain the English translation in Genesis 22: 2 as "your only son." The phrase "your only son" is used not because Abraham had no other son, but because Isaac was the solitary son remaining at home. Notwithstanding, if the Qur'an utilized in this study has erroneously translated the Arabic name *Ishmael* into English as the name *Isaac*, then the contention seems to have substance. Strong emotions would indeed be aroused. Perhaps the point is not necessarily related to which son was presented for sacrifice. It might make more sense to consider what is not being contested. In other words, Abraham was being tested by God. This point is agreed upon by the three major Abrahamic religions. It seems that no one is arguing the testing of Abraham by God.

When arguing about which son was actually presented for sacrifice, an important point seems to get overlooked. Was Abraham the only one being tested in this scenario? Abraham's son was being tested as well. Either son would have been familiar with the sacrificial process, yet the son willingly submitted in faith. Either son, Ishmael or Isaac, would have quickly realized they were about to be offered as a sacrifice. Submitting to that required the same type of faith that Abraham demonstrated when he assured the two helpers, "I

---

[75]   Jay P. Green Sr., *The Interlinear Bible*, Hebrew-Greek-English; 2nd ed. (Peabody, MA: Hendrickson, 1986); Francis Brown et al., *Hebrew and English Lexicon* (Peabody, MA: Hendrickson, 2001).

and the lad will . . . return." By faith, Abraham knew that somehow, someway, God would have him return with his son. God had previously acknowledged that such faith was credited as righteousness. In other words, it establishes the intimacy that only family can provide. It was not the physical makeup of a man that God considered perfect. It was the trust that a child has in his father that God considered perfect. It is the intimacy that family provides. The physical man is the tangible, and the trust is the intangible. This reflects the previous illustration regarding the tangible character of God's promise in contrast to the intangible character of His covenant.

A similar *righteous resulting faith* seemed to have been demonstrated by Hagar in chapter 4. There is a strong argument to say that Abraham's son (whether Ishmael or Isaac) also demonstrated that same *righteous resulting faith*. Perhaps the son's faith was just as instrumental in his ransom (Surah 37:107) as was Abraham's faith. In all three examples, the qualifier was faith. It was not related to the promise of any material thing. The demonstration of unquestionable faith in Him is what matters to God. God desired both Ishmael and Isaac to grasp that faith. Unquestionable faith in Him is what God desires from all mankind. Perhaps God was not only testing Abraham and Isaac but every person who hears or reads this historical account. Whether someone reads this account in the Qur'an or the Bible is not the point. Grasping this faith and establishing family intimacy with Him is what matters to God. In other words, a reader of either Book may never remember the names involved, but if they remember and grasp the message of faith, they have pleased God. That is the intimacy He is looking for with His children. As mentioned, it is demonstrated at birth. Neither the mother nor father expects the suckling infant to earn the right to feed from the mother's breast. The child does not question the source that sustains it. There is no thought involved for either infant or parent. The understanding is a given. Trust in God should manifest as naturally as does an infant suckling from a mother's breast. It should manifest as naturally as the infant's need for the doctor to jump-start their lungs at delivery. God provides the breath and the air. It does not come from Abraham, Ishmael, or Isaac.

It is recorded in Genesis 22:15-18: "Then the angel of the LORD called to Abraham a second time . . . 'because you have done this thing and have not withheld your son . . . I will greatly bless you, and I will greatly multiply your seed . . . In your seed all the nations of the earth shall be blessed.'" Abraham's seed, as well as all the nations of the earth, includes both Ishmael and Isaac. Both are promised to become great nations. God promised that all nations would be blessed. He did not preclude Muslim, Arab, or Jew. In other words, God intimately and equally blessed both Ishmael and Isaac. The biblical record supports that God does not show favoritism. Deuteronomy 10:17 reveals, "For the Lord your God . . . does not show partiality nor take a bribe." In Exodus 23:2-3, God instructs that "you shall not . . . testify in a dispute so as to turn aside after a multitude in order to pervert justice; nor shall you be partial to a poor man in his dispute." Proverbs 11: 1 states, "A false balance is an abomination to the LORD, but a just weight is His delight." It would appear that God wants the land shared by His children, just as any parent would want each of their offspring to dine with them at the family table. How should this sharing operate in society?

In Numbers 34:2, God instructs Moses, "Command the sons of Israel and say to them, ' . . . Canaan . . . is the land that shall fall to you as an inheritance." In Numbers 34:13, "Moses commanded the sons of Israel . . . 'this is the land that you are to aportion . . . among you as a possession.'" The word *possession* implies an expected duty of care, inclusive of custodial stewardship, proper utilization, maintenance, and repair. It is often an exhaustive and expensive responsibility, demanding self-sacrifice in many cases. Being put in charge does not necessarily come with a license to lord over in a self-serving, tyrannical manner. For example, an older sibling may be eager to be put in charge when parents go out for the evening. Not surprisingly, after the first time babysitting, they fully understand the extra effort that is required. They may not be as eager to babysit the next time. The sibling in charge is left responsible to make sure the needs of the household are provided and managed well. Place this back into the context of inheriting an entire territory, and it does not take much imagination to appreciate the demand involved to care for all Abraham's descendants. Both Ishmael's and Isaac's descendants are included in this grouping. Considering how overwhelming it must be, those in charge might end up wishing it were the other way around. Another illustration is a landlord having possession of the property on which the tenant lives. There is an exhausting obligation of care. Many people would rather rent and leave all the aggravation and headaches to the landlord. Descendants of the son who was promised the land might end up wishing they did not have the responsibility. Sometimes it might be easier to be the one being cared for, rather than the one having the responsibility of care. If all readers were surveyed in this regard, it might not be surprising to find the results split down the middle.

As intimated, if God intends that the land be shared, it would seem to indicate that the covenant is associated with something other than the possession of land. It has been suggested that the covenant is more in line with the intimacy God desires. In Deuteronomy 7:7, God informs the Israelites that He blesses them because of the oath He made to bring them out of bondage in Egypt, and not because they are greater or better than any others. God instructs that there should be one law common for both "him who is native among the sons of Israel and for the alien," as found in Numbers 15:29. In Deuteronomy 1:16, He also instructs to "judge righteously between a man and . . . the alien." Subsequently, in Deuteronomy 9:4, God warns that no one is righteous. Prevailing against opposition only comes because the opposition is more wicked and more unrighteous than the prevailing side. One might rephrase this to say that the lesser of two evils prevails, but both are evil. When a sibling feels they have the right to prevail or that that have more right to a parent than their brethren, the potential for estrangement is enhanced. The same holds true when a sibling is not willing to share. This author has not seen or heard of a child who has not displayed such traits to one degree or another, at one time or another. This seems to be an inherent part of human nature, in other words, "mine, mine, mine."

Because of Abraham's lineage to Noah's son Shem, it can be argued that both Jews and Arabs share an ancestry to the Semitic-speaking people. The genetic division is reflected in the definition of *Hebrew*: "A member or descendant of a Semitic people claiming descent from Abraham, Isaac and Jacob; an Israelite; a Jew."[76] The Muslim faith claims roots back to Abraham through Ishmael and not Isaac. Judaism is distinguished by other characteristics as well. It is "the religion, philosophy, and way of life for the Jewish people . . . the expression of the covenantal relationship God established with the Children of Israel . . . The Hebrews / Israelites were already referred to as 'Jews' in later books of the Tanakh [Bible] such as the Book of Ester, with the term *Jews* replacing the title 'Children of Israel.'" Judaism includes "those born Jewish and converts to Judaism . . . the Hebrew God is . . . concerned with the actions of humankind . . . Jews are to imitate God's love for people." However "for some, observance of Jewish law is more important then belief in God per se." In other words, some merely do not believe in "a personified deity active in history" while others feel someone can earn their place at God's family table by strict adherence to the law. However, is there anyone capable of perfect adherence to even the most trivial matters of law? If no one is perfect, then sooner or later, each person will violate the law because of differing views. Differing views are recognized within Judaism. "Judaism lacks a centralized authority . . . variations on the basic beliefs are considered within the scope of Judaism."[77] However, Judaism

> universally recognized the Biblical Covenant between God and . . .
> Abraham as well as the additional aspects of the Covenant revealed
> to Moses . . . in . . . Judaism's more than 3,000-year history . . . Jews
> have experienced slavery, anarchic and theocratic self-government,
> conquest, occupation, and exile; . . . influenced by ancient Egyptian,

[76] *The Free Dictionary*, s.v. "Hebrew," accessed March 2013, http://www.thefreedictionary.com/Hebrew.html.

[77] *Wikipedia, the free encyclopedia*, s.v. "Judaism," accessed April 2013, http://en.wikipedia.org/wiki/Judaism.html.

Babylonian, Persian, and Hellenic cultures, as well as modern . . . Enlightenment . . . Jewishness disrupts the very categories of identity, because it is not national, not genealogical, not religious, but all of these, in dialectrical tension . . . the Reform movement has maintained that a Jew who has converted to another religion is no longer a Jew, and the Israeli Government has also taken that stance . . . However . . . Jews who have converted under duress may be permitted to return to Judaism 'without any action on their part but their desire to rejoin the Jewish community . . . what determines Jewish identity in the State of Israel . . . is still not settled, and occasionally resurfaces in Israeli politics . . . Most Jewish Israelis classify themselves as 'secular' . . . and . . . This portion . . . largely ignores organized religious life.[78]

The Israelites had encountered a number of enemies in their ancient history. The Moabites were already mentioned in chapter 4. The Midianites can be found in Joshua 13:21, and again with "the Amalekites and the sons of the east" in Judges 6:3; 8:1, 24, where it is also discovered that Ishmaelites are considered sons of the east. Amorites, Perizzites, Canaanites, Hittites, Girgashites, Hivites, and Jebusites are mentioned in Joshua 24:11, in addition to Philistines and Amorites in Judges 10:7-8. Anyone watching the media realizes that to this day, Israel has many who seek to harm them. "At around 520 BC, Zechariah predicted:[79] ' . . . when the siege is against Jerusalem, it will also be against Judah [the Jews] . . . in that day I will make Jerusalem a burdensome stone for all the peoples . . . all the nations of the earth will be gathered [for war] because of it' (Zech. 12:2-3)."

---

[78] *Wikipedia, the free encyclopedia*, s.v. "Judaism," accessed April 2013, http://en.wikipedia.org/wiki/Judaism.html.

[79] Hal Lindsey, *The Everlasting Hatred* (Washington, DC: WND Books, 2011), 223.

CHAPTER SIX

THE RADICAL FAMILY ADDITION

In Surah 62:6, the Qur'an warns, "Say: 'O you Jews, if you claim that you are the favorites of God apart from all men, then wish for death.'" If it is true that God does not show favoritism, then the Qur'an seems to make a good point. Compare this to Genesis 17:19 where God informs Abraham, "Sarah . . . will bear you a son . . . Isaac; and I will establish My covenant with him . . . for his descendants after him." Does this mean Ishmael has been excluded from the covenant and that God is showing favoritism? In Genesis 17:20 God clarifies that "as for Ishmael . . . I will bless him, and will make him fruitful and will multiply him exceedingly." It is completely against God's nature to break a promise. Surah 2:80 assures that "Allah will not fail to perform His promise" while 1 Kings 8:56 agrees that "not one word has failed of all His good promise." The promise to Ishmael's descendants cannot go unfulfilled. God desires Ishmael's descendants at His family table as much as He does anyone else. It therefore makes sense that the covenant translates to a method of gaining access to God's family table. Perhaps the method has nothing to do with genealogy or physical lineage. An illustration might help to elaborate this submission.

When a brick is dropped on someone's foot, the result is pain. If someone is hit in the nose, the result is pain. In both instances, a physical action imposed on a physical object results in physical pain. Is a broken heart painful? Do people suffer a painful loss when a loved one passes on? Is a romantic breakup painful? Is the pain of a broken heart felt because a brick has been dropped on it or because someone punched it? Nothing physical happened to the heart and yet immense pain results. There is a nonphysical part of each person that feels that pain. That same nonphysical part of each person is the specific part of them that is designed to share intimacy with God. A person can gain access to God's family table via that nonphysical part of their being. This is the key ingredient to God's covenant with mankind. It does not involve physical land or property.

There is another way to illustrate this idea. The Qur'an states, "He brings them out of the darkness into the light" (Surah 2:257), and "He may bring you forth out of utter darkness into the light" (Surah 33:43). The Bible identifies the LORD as light and salvation (Psalm 27:1). In Acts 26:16-17, God instructs the reader to "witness . . . to . . . people . . . to open their eyes so that they may turn from darkness to light." Darkness cannot exist in the presence of light. When the sun comes up, night becomes day because the darkness ceases to exist. In a sealed, windowless room, it is impossible to see anything, no matter how much someone's eyes adjust to the darkness. This includes perfection. It cannot be seen in the dark. Perfection is required in the presence of God. When the light switch is turned on, light eradicates the darkness, and perfection can be seen. As submitted in chapter 2, each child is born with a nature of darkness. What is the switch that changes human imperfection into perfection? What can change mankind's darkness into light?

Chapter 17 of Genesis speaks of both a covenant and a promise. The covenant in Genesis 17:7 is "to be God to you and your descendants." This implies intimacy. Intimacy is also implied in Surah 19:60-61: "Those who repent . . . and do the right. These will enter Paradise . . . In the gardens of Eden promised by Ar-Rahman." The promise seems to be a location while the covenant seems to be a method to enter what was promised. Genesis 17:8

ys, "I will give to you and to your descendants . . . all the land of Canaan for an everlasting possession." The covenant is intimacy with God while the promise is possession of land. The possession of land is to all Abraham's descendants, which includes both Ishmael and Isaac and the other offspring from his concubines mentioned later in Genesis 25:6. For example, God confirms Ishmael is a descendant in Genesis 21:14. For the most part, parents give possessions to children with the hope that their generosity will reflect well on themselves as parents. In a similar manner, it makes sense that God's intention is that the land be shared. Estrangement in the midst of His family hinders the manifestation of that intention. There is a major flaw if acceptance to God's table is based on the promise rather than the covenant.

The covenant was represented by male circumcision, as instructed by God in Genesis 17:10. In Genesis 17:11, 14, God confirms that the circumcision is merely a sign of the covenant, somewhat similar to branding livestock. The sign merely represents the intimacy God desires. This includes Ishmael, who was circumcised in Genesis 17:23. Why then does God say, "But my covenant I will establish with Isaac," in Genesis 17:21? Did God intend that only descendants of Isaac gain access to His family table? If so, then why would Abraham have gone to the bother of circumcising Ishmael? If Genesis 17:21 originally contained the name *Ishmael* and Judaism skewed it to read *Isaac*, the question remains the same: did God intend to exclude a line of descendants? It appears this matter deserves a closer look.

A branding iron burned into the hide of livestock is not a leash or tether. The livestock can wander off. A family pet can also wander off despite the modern-day branding of collar and tag. Ordinarily, a pet is cared for with tenderness, and an intimate bond develops between the pet and owner. A pet may wander off, but it maintains that desire for tender care. If the pet cannot return home, it responds favorably to a finder who assumes the role of caregiver. If this were not so, dogs and cats would be incapable of transfer to a new family. Another example is sheep. In a one-on-one manner, shepherds shear wool and also tend to wounds. Typically this includes tender reassurance in the shepherd's voice. The sheep equates that voice to the tenderness it desires, and it responds to that particular voice. This is a form of intimacy. The sheep (or pets) are thankful for the care and eagerly submit to the lordship of the shepherd. An outward branding is not what established the intimacy. It is not what preserves the sheep's desire to remain. Because of the bonding, any estrangement is readily avoided or quickly resolved. In the book of Colossians in the New Testament, the apostle Paul refers to being "circumcised with a circumcision made without hands" (Colossians 2:11). It is sometimes referred to as a circumcision of the heart. Simply put, it is the bonding with God that results from being thankful for God's provision. The tender experience is pleasing, and a person grows eager to submit to more tenderness that only God's lordship can provide.

Not everyone agrees with this, and that is fine. This study has found nothing that indicates people must have this idea forced upon them. The Bible, from which this idea is presented, does not support forcing this idea. It is not uncommon, however, to hear complaints of hypocrisy regarding those who claim to follow this submission. Rather than respect a differing view, the presenter will often go to extremes to get their point across or to win an argument, or they fling condescending accusations toward any resistance, and irritation rather than intimacy results. Estrangement sets in before any thought of mutual benefit might occur.

The mutual benefit is salvation. It is reconciliation with God as found throughout the Bible and reflected in Islam's Mahdi. The New Testament identifies the Messiah to be Jesus. But this would need to be confirmed beyond any reasonable doubt and, obviously, is much easier said than it is achieved. God would be a harsh god if He did not provide people with a means to know if and when they are being deceived. The Messiah's lineage to King David was one of the indicators (Isaiah 9:7). This is not an implication that the line of one son is superior to the line of another. No one is denied the opportunity to reconcile with God despite their culture, race, nationality, or imperfections. As far as this study can discern, every living person, including this author, has imperfections that require covering. This is the basis for the need of a Mahdi, a Messiah. To avoid deception, there had to be a sufficient number of indicators fulfilled in such an exact manner, that identification of the Mahdi/Messiah could not be attributed to coincidence. Identification of the Messiah upon His arrival had to be foolproof. This will be discussed further in chapter 9.

The combination of indicators is extremely complex, yet it pales in comparison to the complexity of God Himself. God is infinite, and the human mind cannot grasp infinity. Yet God revealed just enough about Himself to enable mankind to reestablish intimacy with Him. For example, one thing all people can understand is the parent-child relationship. Even children who have never known their parents see other children in families. They come to understand the parent-child relationship by adoption or observation. God used this understanding of the parent-child relationship to illustrate the intimacy that can be enjoyed with Him. The intimacy manifests as a father and a son and the bond between them. The bond is the Holy Spirit. God was not and is not required to reveal anything about Himself. Yet He did so because He desires a family. God has revealed to mankind the "how" of bonding with Him. God injected His desire for family into the heart of mankind. Humans desire family because that is how God chose to multiply His family. It is how God shares His love. Humans can not create love; they can only pass it on (Surah 5:54; 20:39; 28:56; and Jer. 31:3; Rom. 5:5).

Despite the illustration, God remains perfect, and mankind is not. If no one is perfect then how does imperfection cross the border into the realm of perfection? In other words, how does someone sneak into heaven to sit at God's family table? There are many known examples that illustrate someone being sneaked across a border or past a checkpoint or to the other side of a wall or fence. Some were hidden under hay in a wagon. Anyone old enough to remember drive-in movies may know friends who hid someone under a blanket to avoid having to pay that admission fee for that person. Even if hidden in the trunk of the car, once inside the drive-in, they would exit the darkness and rejoin the family. Some have crossed borders through tunnels. That tunnel is covered by earth. A covering is always required.

Consider a pristine white shirt that got stained from coffee, blueberry, ink, and grass. Anyone who has had any one of these stains and then suffered an abrasion will have noticed how their bloodstain overpowered any of the other stains. The only stain visible was the bloodstain. If there is no perfect blood available, then the blood covering the original stain is imperfect. In chapter 2, it was reasoned that each person has a natural tendency to try and cover wrongdoing and imperfection. This illustrates the Bible's account for shedding innocent blood to cover the wrongdoing, in other words, to cover sin. Although remaining imperfect, at least the sin was covered. But this method was only temporary until a perfect covering became available. Animals sacrificed were not perfect because God is the standard of perfection required. In a radio broadcast during September 2013, Dr. David Jeremiah pointed out that obedience is another necessary ingredient for the sacrificial shedding of blood. Animals were led to sacrifice and not given a choice to obey (*Turning Point*, San Diego, CA, Sept. 2013). While listening to the broadcast, J. Grathmore realized that even the leaves covering Adam and Eve had no choice but to obey and die. Unlike the leaves, however, a judge enjoys the freedom to choose. The judge can serve the offender's time in jail and pay the offender's penalty. The penalty is death because just like the leaves, life must be sacrificed to provide the covering. God is the only perfect thing, and the only perfect judge. But how can the eternal God die to provide that perfect blood covering as well as pay the penalty? The Father, Son, and Holy Spirit (triune) relationship provided the answer. God had to become a life that could be sacrificed. The mortal portion of God's life was Jesus. He has returned to the immortal and is believed by Messianic Jews and Christians, that He is soon to return and provide immortality to all God's family. This triune nature is found in both the Old and New Testaments. The Hebrew word for *one* in Deuteronomy 4:6 is

Elohim, where the—*im* suffix gives it a plural meaning. It is the same plural meaning used in Genesis when man and woman become one, and even prior to that when making man "in Our image."[80] Elohim is used again in Psalm 45:6-7 where God is addressing God, and the inference is a plural deity.[81] God dwelled among the Israelites as a cloud of smoke by day, a pillar of fire by night, and amidst the Arc of the Covenant. In other words, a trinity existed, yet all were the same one and only God. A person can be known to others in three distinctly different ways to three completely different people yet remain the same person. A father can be known to his son in a completely different way than how he is known to and by his wife, the child's mother. The mother can have a sister with children, and the niece or nephew knows that father as uncle and has a different perspective than the wife or child. That father may have a father still alive and is known as completely different to that father than he is to his wife, child, nephew, or niece. In each case, that man serves three distinctly different functions. Many people act differently depending on the group they are associating with at the time. It is not uncommon that a parent, wife, niece, child, friend, and coworker of a man, each disagree as to what that man's personality is like. Yet that man remains one and the same man. If a person can display this, all the more God can.

God was now available in a life that could be sacrificed. According to the New Testament record, religious leaders at the time of Jesus's ministry convinced the Romans that Jesus was a radical threat to the Roman Empire (Luke 23:2, 5, 14). One might say that Jesus was the radical family addition. However, the Romans found no guilt. Alternatively Jesus was convicted by Jewish custom (Luke 23:17; John 18:38-39). He was beaten, crucified, and

---

[80] Jay P. Green Sr., *The Interlinear Bible*, Hebrew-Greek-English; 2nd ed. (Peabody, MA: Hendrickson, 1986); Francis Brown et al., *Hebrew and English Lexicon* (Peabody, MA: Hendrickson, 2001).

[81] Jay P. Green Sr., *The Interlinear Bible*, Hebrew-Greek-English; 2nd ed. (Peabody, MA: Hendrickson, 1986); Francis Brown et al., *Hebrew and English Lexicon* (Peabody, MA: Hendrickson, 2001).

died on the cross (John 19:30). The perfect blood to cover all other stains was available. What made this possible was the miraculous resurrection of Jesus from the dead. It proved He was who He said He was—in other words, God in the flesh with perfect blood. In the person and character of Jesus (the Messiah), God willingly chose to pay the penalty for everyone else, substituting Himself in the place of the guilty (1 Peter 2:24). Stains of imperfection can now be covered with perfection. Crossing the border into God's kingdom is now possible. Not everyone agrees with this, and that does not make them a bad person.

Jesus's internal organs were exposed from the beating He endured. Those who knew and loved Him were heartbroken by this. That is the reality that enables anyone to "know the LORD" (Jer. 31:34) and bond with Him intimately. Jesus should have been dead by the time He willingly went to the cross. It was the imperfection, wrongdoing, and sin of every human being that Jesus's blood was shed to cover. Every human shares accountability because each has sinned, including J. Grathmore Stratus III. Some have argued that this is not fair because God had created man with the ability to sin against Him. That is true. God could have created man without freewill and prevented mankind from ever sinning. But someone who likes chocolate would argue that it was unfair that God created them to only like vanilla. God does not desire robots as children any more than humans do. However, many feel that it is unfair to be punished for something they are not responsible for. In other words, man did not create himself, and God is responsible for man's ability to sin. Perhaps God would counter that argument by saying something like "You are correct, and I assume full responsibility for having created you with the ability to sin against Me. So here is what I am going to do. I will come down from heaven and suffer the punishment for you. Now what is your excuse?" It is an individual realization of what Jesus has personally done for them, that results in a broken heart in that person. Shame and guilt are felt for what they have contributed to. It is intimate. Once again, not everyone agrees with this, and that does not make them a bad person.

The New Testament book of Romans confirms that a genuine request to be forgiven for contributing to Jesus's suffering and death seals the intimacy. This seems almost too easy and therefore too good to be true. But as established in previous chapters, God knows when a heart is being genuine and when it is not. A genuine thankfulness for Jesus's substitutionary sacrifice is what connects human hearts to God's heart. The mere news of His death broke the hearts of those who knew Him. The same is true two thousand years later. News of His horrible beating and death breaks the heart of those who come to know Him. The sacrifice was necessary even if only one person had ever lived (Matthew 12:11). As already mentioned, it is the nonphysical part of each human that feels the pain of a broken heart. Once broken, God can start the healing process in that person. A bonding takes place between God and the person He is nursing back to health. The process is really no different from the bond that grows between a shepherd and sheep, or mother and child when tending to her child's sickness or injury. As the pain from shame and guilt reside, the offender is eager to submit more and more to God's tender lordship.

Submission to Jesus's lordship is inaugurated by genuine remorse and repentance (Matthew 3:8). The submission is outwardly represented by baptism just as the Abrahamic covenant was represented by the outward circumcision of the male flesh. Both are a visible branding of sorts. An illustration might be that the folks branded belong to God's ranch. The branding is baptism. It is the outward sign of the new covenant. As demonstrated in the books of Matthew 3:13-17 and Mark 1:9-10, it is the first step in obedience to God's lordship. It simultaneously symbolizes each believer being buried and resurrecting with Jesus. When someone is buried, they are completely covered. It is not a mere sprinkling of dirt on their remains. The complete immersion also symbolizes the need for a complete covering by His blood to hide the sin stains.

Jeremiah 31:31-34 records God's advanced notice: "Behold, days are coming . . . when I will make a new covenant . . . not like the covenant which they broke . . . But . . . the covenant which . . . I will put . . . within them and on their heart I will write it . . . saying . . . 'Know the LORD,' for they will all know Me, from the least of them to the greatest of them . . . and their sin I will remember no more.'" It is the intimacy of knowing the LORD, not merely knowing about Him, that reserves a seat at the family table. Love is intimate. Ordinarily, when a person realizes they have hurt or harmed someone they love, they experience the onset of genuine remorse for what they have done. There would have been no need for a perfect judge to incur the consequence of someone else's wrong if no one had ever done anything wrong to begin with. Many have come to realize that someone else has suffered a punishment meant for them, and they are overcome with gratitude. The degree of punishment from which they were saved is found in Psalm 22:12-18 and Isaiah 50:6 and 53:4-10. It is also mentioned by contemporary secular historians at that time. This will be discussed later in chapter 9. However, forgiveness is not to be confused with consequence.

There are consequences to all sins (all stains), but a perfect God is more fair and just than the most loving parent on earth. Ordinarily, a parent will warn their child not to touch a hot burner on the stove. Very often the temptation overcomes the child, and they burn their finger despite the warning. The parent forgives the child, but the child incurs a blister. The child has no one to blame but itself for the consequence. In the same way that the loving parent forgives the child and tenderly cares for the blister, God will tend to the blisters in His children. In both cases, healing typically takes time. Until healed, blisters entail a level of pain, but that cannot be blamed on the parent who gave the warning. God is always ready to comfort and heal anyone, but He will never force Himself on anyone.

Followers of this Abrahamic belief system are referred to as Christians, although that term was not coined until a considerable time after the resurrection. A better title would be "believers" or "followers" or even "disciples" as they were first called. This included the twelve apostles of Jesus. Each was Jewish, and each was trained in Jesus's ways for three years by Jesus Himself. This training is called discipleship. Discipleship has been passed down via the universal church, which Jesus manifested via His apostles. God's desire is that all He created ultimately join Him at his family table in paradise. This is reflected in 2 Peter 3:9. The process of discipleship operates toward that end. Not everyone will submit to that idea, and God's heart is broken for those who do not choose to join Him. It is not completely different from parents in today's world. No one knows the day or time anyone is going to die. Parents continue to have children even though they don't know if their child may one day be lost to disease, violence, or a tragic accident. God knows He will lose some children as well, but that is because of the individual's free will to reject His covering. God will not force His covering on anyone. No parent would want their child to love them because the child was forced to do so. To begin with, human nature seems to respond with resistance to anthing that is forced upon them. Major corporations spend millions of dollars annually to train managers in dealing with resistance to change.

There are many folks who do not want anything to do with God. It is often viewed as cruel or brutal when something is forced on people. If someone does not want to be with God, it would be cruel to force them to join God at His family table. If they are not going to join God's family, then there must be somewhere else for them to go. In Daniel 12:2, the other place is identified as "everlasting contempt," which, of course, means an eternity of no hope and no intimacy. Surah 4:56 informs, "Those who disbelieve . . . shall be cast into Hell." Even if hell were not a literal location of burning, an eternity of no hope and no intimacy might be just as painful.

The matters of disease, violence, and tragic accidents have been raised and, in fairness, should be addressed. If God is so tender and forgiving, why would He allow such things? The answer relates to perspective. With the exception of the Messiah, this study has been unable to find any example of a perfect person. The question is not related to what God has allowed. Rather, the question relates to what each person can be saved from. Jesus's beating and crucifixion already demonstrates part of it. Warnings of consequences to mankind's wrongdoings are found throughout the Old and New Testaments. Despite the natural and man-made disasters already experienced, God has vividly described events that far exceed anything that even Hollywood might conjure up. According to a TV program devoted entirely to weather, scientists are referencing a coming environmental destruction. They are not radical, religious, or doomsday fanatics but highly revered scientists. Terms such as *global warming* are also prevalent. Whatever anyone desires to call it, the truth is that God foretold it will happen. The alternative to disaster worse than anything ever experienced or imagined is the pleasure of reserving a seat at God's table.

It was submitted earlier in this chapter that in Acts 26:16-17, God instructs the reader to "witness . . . to . . . people . . . to open their eyes so that they may turn from darkness to light." Witnessing is essentially a form of inviting. Imagine proud great-great-grandparents eager for the Thanksgiving when all five generations will finally eat together. Months in advance they advise everyone that an entire banquet hall is reserved and an overabundance of food will be ready. Their only instruction is, "Invite as many to come join us as you can. Start with the first person you see, no matter how they look, talk, smell, dress or believe. Do not be forceful or haughty, and if anyone says no, then merely ask the next person you see. Bring as many along with you as you can when you come to Thanksgiving." This illustration is not necessarily an over simplification of the Great Commission found in Matthew 28:19, 20, as it might seem. According to Scripture, it is the principle, the faith, and the rock upon which the Messiah has built His church (Mt. 16:18). According to this third major faith system, an eternity of happiness is already sealed, and this life is merely the time to extend invitations for others to join the feast in heaven. There are several warnings in the guiding New Testament against false prophets who would have folks *place the cart before the horse*, looking for happiness as the focus of life on this side of heaven. That is not the Gospel as presented by the God inspired New Testament scribes. The Gospel is more about bringing as many others as one can to that place of eternal happiness. Many of the very first Christians were eaten alive by wild beasts in barbaric arenas, and it ironically served to help bring others to that place of eternal happiness when their life on this earth completed. If they had happiness as their goal for this life, they would certainly be viewed as huge failures. It is because happiness was not their goal for this life that makes them winners. Albeit extreme, they were true examples of the *living sacrifice* each follower is called to make (Rom. 12:1, 2). Common opportunities for making a living sacrifice arise each time a follower encounters someone in physical, emotional, or spiritual need. J. Grathmore Stratus III has heard it said somewhere that no one gets to heaven and regrets it.

CHAPTER SEVEN

WHY CAN'T WE ALL
JUST GET ALONG?

Consider the discussion in chapter 4. There is good reason to suspect that the existing estrangement within the family of Abraham's God results more from Sarah's emotions than it might from any bad feeling between Ishmael and Isaac. Barbara LeBey observed that "not to be in contact . . . with a brother . . . is a profound loss, . . . because our families are so deeply related to our sense of who we are."[82] Ishmael was forced to depart the company of his younger brother Isaac. Perhaps he resented being denied the natural tendency to be the protective big brother. It is reasonable to suspect that each brother maintained a degree of pining for the other. Upon the death of Abraham, both Isaac and Ishmael buried their father (Genesis 25:9). Three verses prior to that mention, sons of Abraham's concubines are introduced. Why are those brothers not joining Ishmael and Isaac to bury their father? Apparently, there was a special bond between the two sibling patriarchs that was not shared with the other brothers. It does not appear as though Ishmael and Isaac hated one another. Something has happened to bring about the hatred that now exists between their respective descendants. All in all, there seems to be some hope. In Surahs 3:63, 64, and 71, the following appeal is made: "O people of the Book, let us come to an agreement . . . that we worship no one but God . . . why dispute

---

[82]   Barbara LeBey, *Family Estrangements* (Atlanta, GA: Longstreet Press, 2001).

about Abraham . . . ?" Surah 17:104 states that after drowning Pharaoh, "we told the children of Israel: 'Dwell in the land,'" so why is there now a dispute about who should dwell in the land? In the Bible, Ezekiel 47:22 reads, "You shall divide . . . for an inheritance among yourselves and among the aliens who stay in your midst, who bring forth sons in your midst. And they shall be to you as the native-born among the sons of Israel; they shall be allotted an inheritance with you among the tribes of Israel." The original Hebrew words used in that verse refer to those who dwell as a newcomer and share similar rights.[83] In view of these records from both sides of the dispute, the holy book of each belief system recognizes the right of the other to use the land. On what grounds, then, is the dispute based? Why does each side focus on differences between them? What makes each so repulsive to the other? What changes can be made to restore the bond that compelled Ishmael and Isaac to stand in unity to bury their father Abraham? In the Bible, Colossians 3:10-11 refers to a "new self . . . renewed . . . according to the image of the One who created him . . . in which there is no distinction between . . . circumcised and uncircumcised, barbarian . . . slave and freeman." If this ideal was practiced, could it restore that harmony? What could make the respective sides grasp this ideal, or is the dysfunction beyond hope?

Imagine a family where each member functions properly in their respective role. Conversation among them is transparent, no secrets exist, and no one holds a grudge. Then one day, the wealthy family patriarch passes away, and the family attends the reading of their loved one's last will and testament. Anxiety and tension rise where they never previously existed. Each family member hopes for a comfortable portion of the inheritance. What did the patriarch want done with his possessions? Imagine the sweaty palms as folks anxiously await their fate.

---

[83] Jay P. Green Sr., *The Interlinear Bible*, Hebrew-Greek-English; 2nd ed. (Peabody, MA: Hendrickson, 1986); and Francis Brown et al., *Hebrew and English Lexicon* (Peabody, MA: Hendrickson, 2001).

Now imagine God's last will and testament. God even titled His Bible with the word *Testament*, both the Old and the New. What is His will? What does God want done with His possessions? When is God going to die so His last will and testament can be read? Which family member will get the most important and most valuable possessions? What are those possessions? These thoughts are the background to another point of contention in the family of Abraham's God.

The executor of a person's will is "charged with protecting . . . property until all debts . . . have been paid, and seeing that what's left is transferred to the people who are entitled to it."[84] Notice that debts must first be paid. There is neither possession of land nor inheritance of covenant without first paying any debt. Debt is a penalty of sorts. Reasonable questions regarding the hostile contention between Abraham's descendants would include this: has the debt been paid and who was supposed to pay it? The executor must not entertain any favoritism. Execution requires placing duties in a higher priority than any self-motives: "it does require the highest degree of . . . impartiality . . . to act . . . on behalf of someone else."[85] This contention between Abraham's descendants seems to be inherently flawed. First Samuel 12:22 can be misinterpreted as God showing favoritism toward the Israelites: "The LORD has been pleased to make you a people for Himself." But for what purpose has God done this? His purpose must be according to His last will and testament. As already submitted, His will is to enjoy intimacy with all He created. Each person has been provided an opportunity for inclusion. In this Bible verse and others similar to it, as well as the Surah's previously mentioned, God is simply saying that He has given the Jews the burden of executor for His will. By definition,

---

[84] Mary J. D. Randolph, *NOLO Law for ALL*, "What Does an Executor Do?" accessed September 2013, nolo.com/legal-encyclopedia/what-does-executor-do-30236.html.

[85] Mary J. D. Randolph, *NOLO Law for ALL*, "What Does an Executor Do?" accessed September 2013, nolo.com/legal-encyclopedia/what-does-executor-do-30236.html.

"the executor holds legal title to the estate property, but may *not* use the title or property for his/her own benefit, unless permitted by the terms of the will."[86] It has already been submitted that the terms of God's will permit (and require) a shared use of the land. It might be argued that non-Jews received the better part of the covenant. To be an executor is "a burden"[87] and "duties also include . . . the ability to . . . be sued."[88] As proposed in previous chapters, the covenant involves faith-based access to God's family table in the land He originally intended for mankind. Adam and Eve were not Jews, Arabs, Muslims, infidels or Gentiles. But like every person alive today, they were guilty of wrongdoing. Their penalty had to be paid and their resulting imperfection covered. This remains true of every person alive today, including the author of this study. It would appear God has chosen the Jews to pay the debt. Perhaps this idea would bring things full circle from the discussion regarding Genesis 17:19, 21: "Isaac . . . I will establish My covenant with him . . . My covenant I will establish with Isaac." The covenant would establish the method by which all mankind would be given the opportunity to reconcile with God and sit at His family table for all eternity. The method would pay all the debt and cover all the imperfection. The covenant requires the sacrifice of innocent life. That does not sound like something people would want to fight to obtain. This seems like something a logical mind would fight to avoid. It seems more logical that the sides would be fighting in reverse of what they are now.

Reverse scenarios are not uncommon in mankind. Early in his career, J. Grathmore navigated oceangoing cargo ships to foreign shores. His shipping routes always took him to lands of immense devastation and despair, while

---

[86] *Wikipedia, the free encyclopedia,* s.v. "Executor," accessed September 2013, http://en.wikipedia.org/wiki/Executor.html.

[87] Mary J. D. Randolph, *NOLO Law for ALL,* "What Does an Executor Do?" accessed September 2013, nolo.com/legal-encyclopedia/what-does-executor-do-30236.html.

[88] *Wikipedia, the free encyclopedia,* s.v. "Executor," accessed September 2013, http://en.wikipedia.org/wiki/Executor.html.

his peers would come home with stories of long stays in ports offering all the pleasures a young man could imagine. What made it seem even more desirable was the lack of competition for those pleasures. When a navy ship lands, hundreds of men compete for the "pleasures" in port. That competition is reduced to a handful of merchant mariners for a cargo ship. Although this seemed unfair to him, J. Grathmore contemplated why he never seemed to get that voyage to pleasure. Perhaps it was because the God of Abraham was preparing him to conduct this study. What he found each time he returned to the USA was a reverse scenario. Those he had seen devastated and without hope fought with every last ounce of strength to hang on to life. Yet in the land of abundance, so many people with so much to live for were committing suicide. In other words, without proper perspective and humility, a blessing can easily become a curse. Imagine after thousands of years of contention, and years of fighting, and loss of life, the winner finds that all they won was a curse. Perhaps there is something to be said regarding the often-heard expression "be careful what you pray for." Perhaps mankind should be careful what it fights for.

Despite their points of contention, both nations have made wondrous contributions to society. Islam enjoys noted acclaim for architecture, calligraphy, painting, and ceramics. It might be safe to assume that at one time or another, almost everyone has seen the beauty of a magnificent Persian rug or carpet. Although the intellectual game of chess was founded in India, it was Muslims who introduced it to Europe. It was the Islamic influence in medieval Europe that contributed to and preserved medicine, agriculture, music, and ancient texts such as those from Aristotle. Christian scholars such as Leonardo Fibonacci, Adelard of Bath, and Constantine the African conducted many of their scientific studies in Muslim nations. The mentioned Leonardo Fibonacci introduced the mathematical method of algorism to Europe. It was developed by the Persian al-Khwarizmi. After the fall of the Roman Empire, cherished classical texts were preserved and translated in Baghdad. In his writings regarding optical science, Isaac Newton included references from Ibn al-Haytham.

> As Professor Victor J. Katz writes: " . . . in Europe . . . the first algebra works . . . were translations of . . . Islamic authors." The words algorithm . . . from Al-Khwarizmi's Latinized name Algorismi, and algebra . . . Regiomantus . . . took his material on spherical trigonometry (without acknowledgement) from Arab sources . . . Avicenna's *The Canon of Medicine* (1025) . . . remained a standard medical texbook in Europe until the early modern period . . . Muhammad ibn Zakariya Razi (al-Razi) wrote the . . . careful . . . distinction between measles and smallpox . . . Ibn al-Haytham . . . rejected Ptolemy's theory that light was emitted by the eye . . . and was the most significant advance . . . until Kepler . . . The production of sugar from sugar cane, water clocks, pulp and paper, silk and various advances in making perfume, were transmitted from the Islamic world to medieval Europe . . . technologies in the Islamic world . . . adopted in European . . . technology . . . included . . . the astronomical sextant."[89]

According to the firsthand experience of J. Grathmore Stratus III, sextants remained in use as recently as 1978. Perhaps Grathmore was the last of the ancient mariners to use one.

> Contributions from the Jewish descendants are equally worthy. The following are examples:

> Albert Einstein   physicist
> Jonas Salk   created first polio vaccine

---

[89]   *Wikipedia, the free encyclopedia*, "Islamic Contributions to Medieval Europe," accessed March 2013, http://en.wikipedia.org/wiki/Islamic_contributions_to_Medieval_Europe.html.

Galileo	discovered the speed of light
Selman Waksman	discovered streptomycin; coined the word *antibiotic*
Gabriel Lippmann	discovered color photography
Briton Epsein	identified first cancer virus
Maria Meyer	proposed the structure of atomic nuclei
Julius Mayer	discovered the law of thermodynamics
Isaac Singer	invented the sewing machine

Each descendant nation has benefitted from the other. All the Abrahamic religions encourage the practice of giving to the poor and caring for widows and orphans. Each believes in fasting to draw nearer to God, to show God gratitude and develop control over temptations of the flesh. Yet unthinkable violence, brutal devastation, and heartbreaking loss continue to appear daily in the media from the Middle East. Do the respective sides appreciate the contributions each has made to benefit the other? As it stands now, actions of the offspring discredit the legacy of the parent. However, if each tended to the needs of the other, the bonding between Ishmael and Isaac could be revitalized. They already tend to one another's needs, even if by default, as their contributions to society spread across the globe. So why not formalize it and show the world a legacy worth following, rather than a lineage of turmoil? As they did with Abraham, families could once again bury their parents because of old age, rather than because of hate and violence like they do today. Heartbreaking news of car bombings, artlillary fire and border clashes seem to find their way into the media on a regular basis.

A precedent has already been set for this reunion. To review chapter 4, in fear of encountering Esau, Jacob sent gifts ahead with the message that they come from "your servant Jacob; it is a present to my lord Esau" (Genesis 32:18). His fear was intensified because on the night before, Jacob's thigh had been dislocated (Genesis 32:25). Weakened, he was now more dependent on God than ever before. In Genesis 32:28, the Lord changed his name from *Jacob* (meaning "a supplanter" or "con man") to *Israel* (meaning "God rules," "one who strives with God," or "a prince of God").[90] The injury rendered him less able to defend his family from Esau. That morning, as Esau was approaching him, Jacob went forward and stopped seven times to bow to the ground. "Then Esau ran to meet him and embraced him, and fell on his neck and kissed him, and they wept" (Genesis 33:1-4). Prior to this, Esau harbored a strong hate for Jacob. Esau had vowed to kill him. This demonstration seems to indicate that humility is a nesessary ingredient to reconciliation, and someone must take the first step by conceding. It also demonstrates that God expects reliance on Him to change the heart of an adversary. Surrender to and reliance upon Him also precedes God's action to change a person's heart from being adversarial to one that tends to the needs of others. Beginning in Genesis 33:9, both brothers demonstrate such a concern. Esau sums it up in Genesis 33:15 by stating, "'Please let me leave with you some of the people who are with me.' But he [Israel] said, 'What need is there?'"

The hope found in the above record remains heavily challenged. Surah 2:39 states, "Those who deny and reject Our signs will belong to hell." Regarding disbelievers, the instruction in Surah 4:89 is to "seize them wherever they are and do away with them." Surah 9:29 directs Islam to "fight those people of the Book . . . until all of them pay . . . in submission." In the Bible, Psalm 83:4 poses an ominous reading: "They have said, 'Come, and let us wipe them out as a nation, that the name of Israel be remembered no more.'" Because the name Israel continues to be remembered, the passage must refer to the future.

Jihad is the term Muslims use to capture the idea of moral and religious perfection. Unless specifically mentioned in regard to morality and religion, it dons a military connotation. By definition it means "to struggle and/or strive" while it can infer the imposing of one will over another. It is a term debated among Muslims, and some view it as a defensive form of warfare. However,

---

[90]   William MacDonald, *Believer's Bible Commentary* (Nashville, TN: Thomas Nelson, 1995), 68.

military action against non-Muslim positions is the more accepted view.[91] In speculation, perhaps the thought is that if all people on earth followed Islam, moral and religious perfection would finally exist. If so, any resistance would jeopardize the perfection. Taking the speculation to a possible conclusion, it might seem that eradication of any resistance would be justified because world perfection would be achieved. Even in the Bible, God commissioned Abraham, Moses, Joshua, and others to eradicate wickedness. But if the perfection had not been achieved via force previously, why would it work now? Even if every human being submitted willfully, consequence remains for the sins already committed. Imperfect thoughts are seen by God, and imperfection cannot exist at His table. Because thoughts are often imperfect, there are consequences for wrong thoughts as well. No matter how much good might outweigh bad, the bad attaches a penalty. When a reckless driver appears before the judge, that judge does not ask how many good things the driver did leading up to the traffic violation. In a similar manner, controlling all the land and eradicating all nonconformists does not tear down the border that exists between mankind's imperfection and God's perfection. Yet land possession remains a major stumbling block and distracts many on both sides from what God actually desires. More than 2,500 years ago in 520 BC, the prophet Zechariah was shown the conflict that now exists between the descendants from Abraham. He recorded it in this way: "Behold, I am going to make Jerusalem a cup that causes intoxication to all the surrounding peoples; and when the siege is against Jerusalem, it will also be against Judah [the Jews] . . . in that day I will make Jerusalem a burdensome stone for all the peoples . . . And all the nations of the earth will be gathered [for war] because of it." This reading looks like it could have come out of an article from today's newspaper. Both sides seem to be caught up in a territorial matter. They seem to be missing the point God has in mind regarding His covenant. Both sides are being distracted from eternity by that which withers and dies. How can the course of mankind be adjusted back to the ideal world God intended for it? Should it start with a centralized

---

[91]   *Wikipedia, the free encyclopedia*, s.v. "Islam," accessed April 2013, http://en.wikipedia.org/wiki/Islam.html.

world-control to impose a system that it perceives will establish and maintain world peace? If that is a viable option, then why do major corporations go to great expense to manage the workforce response to introduced change? This indicates that human nature simply does not respond in a positive manner to change, especially when the change is forced.

CHAPTER EIGHT

IS RECONCILIATION POSSIBLE?

A common phrase often heard is "A chain is only as strong as its weakest link." A line of descendants is a chain of sorts with people as the links. Political processes, belief systems, and social groups are all comprised of people. Considering that no one is perfect, it might be safe to assume that several weak links exist in all areas of human relations. Weak links are not always the result of inherent qualities. Neglect and lack of maintenance can cause links of iron to weaken. Neglect and insensitivity can cause links of humans to weaken. Anyone who has attended managerial training has learned that motivation is related to needs. Forced change is met with resistance, but satisfying needs propels a motivated staff. A motivated staff makes the boss look good. The staff works toward meeting the corporate goals and objectives, and positive results are achieved. If a chain of people do not operate in unity, the ability to work in unity with other groups is severely hindered. There have been many examples of weak links in the chain descending from Ishmael as well as in the chain descending from Isaac. Perhaps this is why today's media reports so many instances of violence in the Middle East and elsewhere. At times, the reported violence is actually committed among factions within the respective chains. Apparently, internal dysfunction is nothing new.

The Bible book of Numbers 16:2-3 records that "some of the sons of Israel . . . assembled together against Moses" while Judges 20:28 states, "the sons of Benjamin would not listen to the voice of their brothers, the sons of Israel. The sons of Benjamin gathered . . . to battle against the sons of Israel." Readers familiar with the Bible already know how the Israelites later divided into two kingdoms. Treachery existed not only between King David's sons but between the king and his son as well. Major dysfunction in the family existed. It seems the descendants from Ishmael were susceptible to this as well. F. E. Peters records that "Shiite Muslims have accused Sunni Muslims of tampering with the text of the Quran."[92] "There have been many violent conflicts between the Sunni and Shi'as branches of Islam . . . After the 2003 invasion of Iraq by a western coalition there was armed conflict between branches of Islam, with fighting and bombings, even of mosques."[93] Internal division is found in Christianity as well. The island nation of Ireland has provided perhaps the most extreme example. Decades of violence and killing existed between Catholics and Protestants.

Internal division has led to a state of dysfunction among the Abrahamic religions, both internally and externally. Any hope of healing would seem to entail addressing the essence of family estrangement. Diagnosis typically includes looking for "emotional, behavioral, or developmental disorders . . . and . . . problems with . . . family members"[94] along with obtaining insight

---

[92]   F. E. Peters, *The Children of Abraham* (Princeton, NJ: Princeton University Press, 2004), 5.

[93]   *Wikipedia, the free encyclopedia*, s.v. "Abrahamic religions," accessed April 2013, http://en.wikipedia/wiki/Abrahamic_religions.htm.

[94]   The Ohio State University (Wexner Medical Center), "Comprehensive Psychiatric Evaluations," *About Mental Health*, accessed September 2013, http://medicalcenter.osu.edu/patientcare/healthcare_services/mental_health/mental_health_about/about_mental_healthe/comprehensive_psychiatric_evaluations/Page/index.aspx.

into family background.[95] A reader might want to g
2 and then continue this thought. Based upon the
proposed that mankind is not willing to submit to a s
development speaks to this. Infants submit to tende
Interruptions to that intimacy, as well as inappropri
an adverse affect on the child's development. Ev
systems imposed on them. Depending on how intim
child's development, a degree of negative response is
Submission does not seem to come naturally. Childr
a natural tendency to want to rebel. It is not likely t
will succeed eternally. But what other option is th
unity? Is there an effective system that commences
productive citizenship? Perhaps it can be found by fu
background of the estranged family of Abraham's G

In this study, the family background begins wit
chapter 3, all Abrahamic religions worship God as
Qur'an states, "He is *All-powerful*" in Surah 42:29 whil
"There is no changing His laws. He is all-hearing and
Surahs back this up: "Allah has never changed" (8:
be changed" (50:29), and "There is no changing the
The Bible agrees in Deuteronomy 4:2: "You shall not
am commanding you, nor take away from it." In Psal
"I will not . . . alter the utterance of My lips." Accor
and the Bible, God is certainly powerful enough to ens
every generation, thereby never requiring anyone to co
to correct it. Both books claim that God's Word has a
will remain perfect throughout all generations—past, p
human or even angelic effort to change it, rewrite it, ad
reinvent it, or even correct it will be thwarted by God

---

95 Jane Framingham, "What is Psychological Assessmen
    2013, http://psychcentral.com/lib/what-is-psychological-

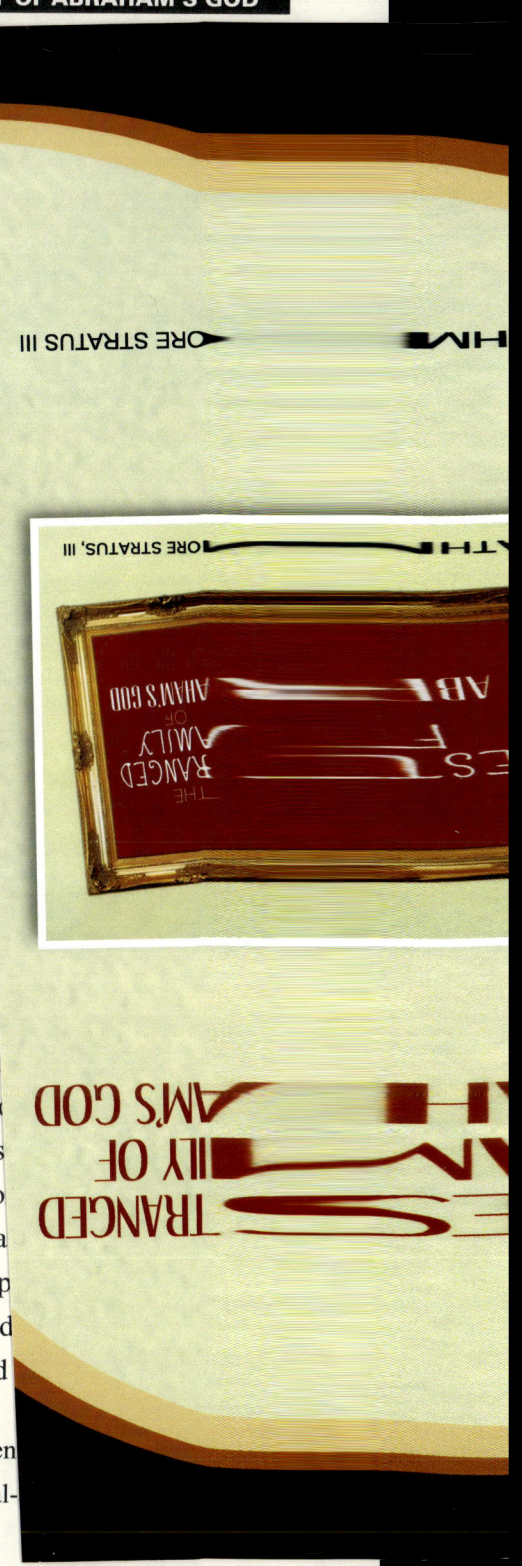

correction means that God was wrong and fallible. To the contrary, both the Qur'an and the Bible teach that God is infallible. A logical conclusion would be that an adherent of either book would be contradicting their faith to think, speak, or write otherwise. Either God is all-powerful, or He is not. Considering the Qur'an was written some 2,700 years after Abraham, perhaps God did use the Qur'an to correct errors in the first recording of His Word, the Bible. This raises the question, is the Bible reliable and accurate?

The ability to write and preserve what was written had been a well-established practice, which enabled Moses to record the Bible's first five books. The Code of Hammurabi was written in 1750 BC and was discovered in 1901. It confirmed that several systems of writing and law existed at that time. In respect to biblical writers, the requirement for accuracy was paramount, even if it meant self-incrimination. For example, the prophets faced death by stoning if their words did not come true. Meantime, several copies of the original scripture scrolls were meticulously maintained by several scribes. This facilitated a committed system of checks and balances. If one copy wore out and needed replacing, then all copies were transcribed onto new papyrus or parchment simultaneously. This was required even if the other copies remained in good condition. Each letter had to be visually confirmed and the distance between them checked with thread. Each letter was counted and compared to the original. A single mistake on any of the new copies meant the entire replacement had to be destroyed and the process restarted. Discovery of the Dead Sea Scrolls seems to be common knowledge nowadays. They were written more than two hundred years before Christ, and with the exception of Esther, they contained every book of the Old Testament. Modern-day engineers have confirmed that the design and dimensions recorded for Noah's ark are what would be required for a barge of that type in heavy seas. Sanitation and quarantine methods recorded by Moses were utilized to rid Europe of the Black Plague. Previously considered as myths, evidence now proves the existence of Sodom and Gomorrah. People now visit museums of Hittite artifacts, yet it was taught that the Hittites never existed. During an excavation, the walls of

Jericho were found fallen outward from the city. Jacob's well has also been identified, and the water remains potable.[96]

Imagine someone predicting 670 different things will come true, and 668 of them do. It would be reasonable to accept that the last remaining predictions are reliable and will happen. The fact is that in respect of biblical prophecies, "668 are known to be fulfilled, with none ever proved false . . . all unfulfilled prophescies relate to the second coming of Christ and 'end times.'" "There are . . . other prophecies . . . in the lifetime of eyewitnesses. Hence . . . confirmable by those recording them."[97] Historic record has confirmed the fulfillment of the other prophecies.

In respect of the New Testament Gospels, Ralph Muncaster points out that "both the differences and the similarities . . . are . . . indications of trustworthiness. If only similarities existed, a common source might be considered biased . . . If only differences existed, reconciliation could be difficult . . . Similarities and differences of eyewitness testimony lend credibility . . . as it would in a court of law today . . . All Gospels were completed . . . well within the lifetime of eyewitnesses . . . the writing . . . occurred 10 to 35 years after the resurrection." The eyewitness accounts include Jesus's postcrucifixion appearance to as many as five hundred people at one time. Mr. Muncaster further offers that in regard to Sir David Dalrymple, "His exhaustive investigation of other non-Bible writings in existence from the period of AD 100 to AD 300 (overlapping the time of eyewitnesses) revealed that the entire New Testament existed in direct quotes with the exception of only eleven verses."[98]

---

96   Ralph O. Muncaster, *Can You Trust the Bible?* (Eugene, OR: Harvest House Publishers, 2000), 10, 12, 14, 18, 28, 43; Ralph O. Muncaster, *Is the Bible Really a Message from God?* (Eugene, OR: Harvest House Publishers, 2000).

97   Ralph O. Muncaster, *Is the Bible Really a Message from God?* (Eugene, OR: Harvest House Publishers, 2000).

98   Ralph O. Muncaster, *Can You Trust the Bible?* (Eugene, OR: Harvest House Publishers, 2000).

Scientists "have determined that anything beyond one chance in 10 to the 50th power is beyond reason—essentially impossible or absurd . . . . There are 322 prophecies reagarding the Messiah in the old Testament." The odds of one man fulfilling them all are 10 to the 157th power. That is more than three times the realm of impossibility, yet the New Testament verifies Jesus filled them all. This verification was recorded within the lifetime of the eyewitnesses. How do we know today that George Washington was the first president of the United States? It is because of the recorded testimony of the eyewitnesses. Eyewitness records are also found among Jewish rabbis. Although it brought them embarrasement, their dedication to accuracy and truth compelled them to record the Resurrection-related events. Nonrabbitic Jewish historians such as Josephus (circa AD 64-93) also made mention of the events. Non-Jewish recordings include Thallus (circa AD 52), Cornelius Tacitus (AD 64-116), Pliny the Younger (circa AD 112), Hadrian (circa AD 117-138), Suetonius (circa AD 120), Phlegon (circa AD 140), Lucian of Samosata (circa AD 170), and Mara Bar-Serapion (circa AD 70).[99]

The crucifixion of Jesus was described by the prophet Isaiah more than six hundred to seven hundred years before the Romans developed that form of capital punishment. Ralph Muncaster points out that "the crucifixion of Jesus was especially well documented and accepted as fact . . . . Both the absolute death of Jesus and the prevention of a hoax were critical, since Jesus had claimed He would overcome death. Furthermore, He had already raised others from the dead. As a result, all precautions were taken (Matthew 27:62-66) . . . . No one could produce a dead body of Jesus . . . which would have stopped the resurrection story forever. Is a theft of Jesus's body even remotely possible?

- All 16 guards . . . risk the penalty of crucifixion by sleeping or deserting . . .

---

[99] Ralph O. Muncaster, *Is the Bible Really a Message from God?* (Eugene, OR: Harvest House Publishers, 2000), 31, 38, 39; Ralph O. Muncaster, *What Is the Proof for the Resurrection?* (Eugene, OR: Harvest House Publishers, 2000), 14, 16.

- The disciples were in a state of shock, fear and disarray . . . Is it reasonable to think they quickly created a brilliant plan and flawlessly executed it on the Sabbath day of rest?
- . . . stealing the body would have created a lie with no apparent benefit—and death, for no purpose, for the disciples."[100]

The above notwithstanding, this investigation respects anyone's desire to maintain that the Bible has been skewed. However, it does suggest that certain matters might need to be addressed in this regard. At this time, the study merely presents uncertainties and questions that the reader or listener may want to consider.

If attempting to skew the Bible to favor themselves, it doesn't seem to make sense that the Jewish scribes would have mentioned so many atrocities perpetrated by their own people. It is difficult for many people to imagine purposely throwing their flesh-and-blood brother into a dried-up well to die. But that is what Jacob's sons did to their brother Joseph (Genesis 37:24). Moses's role as murderer in Exodus 2:11-15 would have been a likely fact to leave out as well. Consider also the hero status of Caleb. The Calebite Nabal is described as "harsh and evil" in 1 Samuel 25:3-11. If not for the scribes' commitment to accuracy, his repulsive character and offense to David would have been excluded from record. Meanwhile in Judges 13:1, the Jews show themselves as subordinate to their adversaries the Philistines; and in Judges 20:28, they admit to battling among themselves in disunity. They present themselves as idol worshippers in Judges 17. A very interesting example is found in 1 Samuel 27. David is hailed in both the Old and New Testaments as being *a man after God's own heart* (1 Sam. 13:14; Acts 13:22). However, in 1 Samuel 27, the scribes were careful to include two accounts of David that many use to discredit his integrity. The first account records David's barbaric slaughter of three entire communities, leaving no survivors and taking no

---

[100] Ralph O. Muncaster, *How Do We Know Jesus Is God?* (Eugene, OR: Harvest House Publishers, 2000), 20, 21.

prisoners. He then intentionally lied about the identity of those communities. Obviously the scribes' motivation was a devotion to truth rather than a hidden agenda for favoritism. However it would appear that there must be error if David is regarded as a man after God's own heart. The error is dispelled in Psalm 119:29 where David repents for his lies. The record of his lies was necessary to demonstrate God's mercy and forgiveness in response to repentance. The slaughter was the completion of God's instructions to Saul. Saul's failure to execute resulted in David's succession as king (I Sam. 15:3, 9, 11, 17-19, 22, 23: 28:17, 18). Atrocity was also recorded In Jeremiah 32:35, where Israelites are found sacrificing their children to the god Molech. This was recorded to demonstrate the consequence of disobedience, which in this case involved conquest and enslavement of the Jewish nation. The atrocities against God and man that the Jews have recorded about themselves are too numerous to list in this study. Similarly, the New Testament records items that someone would withhold if attempting to promote their position. For example, Moabites were known enemies of the Jews, yet the lineage of the Jewish Messiah contains the Moabite woman Ruth (Matthew 1:6). To incriminate themselves even further, the New Testament's record of Jesus's lineage also includes the harlot Rahab (Exodus 2:1; Matthew 1:5). It was included to demonstrate that the Messiah is savior for all who call upon Him because, according to scripture, all sin is forgiven in response to genuine repentance.

If the goal was to discredit non-Jews, Arabs, and Muslims, then it seems the Jewish scribes failed in that pursuit. There are a number of accolades that go out to the nations just mentioned. The Midianite Jethro is credited with providing Moses the wisdom to govern Hebrew society (Exodus 18:13-27). Isaac had to obtain Aramean permission in order to get married (Genesis 25:20). Isaac's son married Ishmael's daughters (Genesis 28:9). King David's sister married an Ishmaelite (1 Chronicles 2:17). At the Passover Feast, Jews use saltwater to remind them that the joy of their freedom is decreased because their Arab cousins had to suffer the ten plagues in Egypt (Exodus 9:14). Amos 9:7 records that God delivered not only Jews but Philistines as well. The

Hebrews valued the opinion of the Philistines (Ezekiel 16:27). Lot, Ishmael, and Esau all ventured east. Much later, it was magi from the east that came to worship God when He entered into the world as an infant (Matthew 2:1). These records might be a good precedent for reconciling current relations.

Other matters remain to which this study is unable to offer insight. They are presented in the event the reader might be inspired to research further. For example, it is not clear why the descendants of Ishmael did not have their own meticulous means of preserving God's Word when He presented it 2,700 years before the Qur'an. Knowing God had said He would never change His Word, the pre-Islam believers would have had something concrete to check against rather than something skewed. It is unclear from this study why there is contention regarding who "God's chosen people" are because Surah 44:30-32 states, "So We saved the children of Israel . . . And We exalted them over the other people." Surah 2:47 reaffirms this: "Remember, O children of Israel . . . I . . . made you exalted amoung the nations of the world." In a similar manner, Surah 19:58 adds, "These are those who were favored by god . . . the offspring of Abraham and Israel." Israel was the son of Isaac. Surah 6:84 seems to put this to rest in the statement "And we gave him Isaac and Jacob and guided them, as We had guided Noah before them." The matter regarding Christ is somewhat confusing. Surah 5:75 states that "the Christ, son of Mary, was but an apostle." If that is all there is to Christ, then it is unclear why the Qur'an gives so much attention to the virgin birth (Surahs 2:87; 3:45-47; 21:91), while demonstrating Jesus with abilities reserved only for God Himself (Surahs 3:55; 19:20; 21:91). Surah 5:110 credits Jesus: "Out of mire . . . you breathed a new spirit into it," and in Surah 4:171, the Qur'an names him the Messiah. Another uncertainty relates to reports that appeared in the media after the World Trade Center incident on September 11, 2001. Paraphrasing, it was not uncommon to hear that one of the motivations behind the attack involved the promise of seventy virgins in paradise as a reward for that horrific action. This might present some confusion because Surah 32:17 states that "no soul knows what peace and joy lie hidden from them as reward for what they have done." If seventy virgins is the reward, this Surah infers that no one is supposed to know that.

Otherwise, as mentioned, God used the lineage of David to be the executor of His will. It was one of the many prophesies that would be used to confirm the identity of the Messiah when He arrived. If He wanted, God could have used the lineage of Ishmael, but the intention would have been the same. As executor, the Jews have a custodial stewardship to not only maintain the land but to care for the inhabitants as well. The land was meant to be shared just as the food at God's family table in heaven is to be shared. Think back to the illustration of the landlord/tenant covenant. The terms of the contract provide obligations and remedies that ensure the land is mutually beneficial to both parties. Arguably, what someone does with the land is more significant than the possession of the land. Ultimately, all land belongs to God, and He expects both landlord and tenant to treat His property in a manner that reflects loving others as one would love oneself. This is the expected character of an executor, as discussed in chapter 7.

Reconciliation and coexistence are inferred in Surah 3:103: "Remember . . . when you were one another's foe and He reconciled your hearts" as well as in Surah 17:104, "We told the children of Israel: 'Dwell in the land.'" The Bible supports this inference in Ezekiel 47:22: "You shall divide . . . an inheritance . . . among the aliens . . . in your midst . . . and they shall be to you as the native-born among the sons of Israel; they shall be allotted an inheritance with you."

Are there any present-day examples of reconciled cultures? A short ride outside of Philadelphia, Pennsylvania, there resides a living example. A comfortable thirty-minute seating on the PATCO high-speed line provides a pleasant view while crossing the Delaware River into New Jersey. Once out of Camden, it makes several stops in quaint southern New Jersey villages. Those who ride to the end, however, are quick to start their cars and exit the town without haste. Mismanagement from several administrations ago has ravaged the one-time flourishing community. The last few administrations have been working hard to recover from the resulting deteriorations. Through a partnership between the local municipality and a local nonprofit organization called Commitment To Community (CTC), wondrous opportunities are revitalizing hope. Progress is underway, and results are already noticeable. Each month, both audience and artists of all genres remain eager to learn more of styles beyond their own. The Arts Avenue (www.theartsavenue.com) is growing by word of mouth alone, thanks to the sponsorship of CTC and local business. This is possible only because people from all races, cultures, ages and socio-economic strata have been working together in a like-minded fashion. Each has put self aside and committed to a genuine concern for others. An intimate bond in like mind and spirit is accomplishing what was thought to be impossible. It is a proven model to follow. It can succeed at any level, in any location, and at any time in history.

CHAPTER NINE

READER'S CHOICE

The author continues to respect each reader's choice regarding what each one may desire to believe and conclude. However, the proposed formula for reconciliation might be clearer to those who believe God is powerful enough to ensure that His Word has not been skewed. Either way, resources used in this study revealed some key points to help those experiencing estranged family situations. For their benefit, those points have been summarized herein.

It has already been suggested that good outweighing bad does not eliminate the consequence of wrongdoing. Nor does it erase the imperfection necessary to gain access to God's family table. However, this study supports that the healing process for reconciliation starts with God. Intimacy with Him brings healing. One proposal for access to His family table has been the idea of giving one's own life for others. To eradicate the enemy, kamikaze pilots in World War II would sacrifice their lives and willingly crash their plane into United States warships. In September of 2001, jet airliners were crashed into New York's World Trade Center and the Pentagon in Washington, DC. Much of the media reported an association with a belief that sacrificing one's life to eradicate the enemy gained entrance to God's paradise. Hadiths are loosely defined as commentaries to accompany the Qur'an. "The Hadith explicitly states that the Muslim is promised eternal victory in the act of holy war.

Victory includes . . . eternal forgiveness . . . and blessing in Paradise."[101] In John 15:13, the New Testament states, "Greater love has no one than this, that one lay down his life for his friends." It is not certain whether planes flown into warships and skyscrapers were done selflessly to save the life of friends from an enemy, or self-servingly to gain entrance to paradise. The latter would not seem to qualify as laying down one's life for another. It seems the motivation behind the self-sacrifice is what God compares to His standard of perfection. It will determine how the self-sacrifice is judged. It can be selfless, or it can be self-serving. As an example of the latter, the male expectation of female virgins as a reward was already discussed. Speaking to the former, the genuine concern for others with no expectation of reward is the standard of perfection required. Surah 67:14 indicates that God will know the true motive: "Can He who has created not know (His creation)? He is all-penetrating, all-aware." The Qur'an further implies that imperfection cannot exist in the presence of perfection, as found in Surah 2:38, 39: "When I send guidance . . . those who deny and reject . . . will belong to Hell"; and in Surah 9:32, "God . . . wills to perfect his light, however the unbelievers be averse." The Bible agrees with this in Psalm 137:7, 13, "Where can I flee from your presence? . . . You formed my inward parts" and in 2 Corinthians 4:6, "'Light shall shine out of darkness.'"

Christians and Messianic Jews recognize the Messiah presented in Isaiah 9:6 and 7: "For a child will be born to us, a son will be given to us; And the government will rest on His shoulders; And His name will be called Wonderful Counselor, Mighty God, Eternal Father, Prince of Peace. There will be no end to the increase of His government or of peace, On the throne of David and over his kingdom, To establish it and to uphold it with justice and righteousness From then on and forevermore. The zeal of the LORD of hosts will accomplish this." According to Acts 1:9-10, these believers now look for and await the return of this Messiah: "He was lifted up . . . and a cloud received Him out of their sight. And . . . two men in white clothing . . . said, 'Men of Galilee . . . This Jesus . . . will come in just the same way as you have watched Him go into heaven.'"

[101] M. Caner and E. Caner, *Unveiling Islam* (Grand Rapids, MI: Kregel, 2002), 195.

Meanwhile Judaism and Islam look for the coming of the Madhi/Messiah. In *The Children of Abraham*, F. E. Peters observes that "the Quran's thirty-five references to Isa ibn Miryam show an extraordinary regard for Jesus, 'the Messiah,' as it frequently titles him."[102] The author of *The Everlasting Hatred* submits that "Iran's president, Mahmoud Ahmadinejad, is a devout believer in an Islamic prophecy that says the Muslim messiah, known as the 'Mahdi' is ready to return and only awaits the beginning of an Armageddon-type war . . . that will cause him to return and . . . lead the Muslims to world domination.[103]" Regardless of any of the three perspectives, all agree a Messiah is coming. It is not completely beyond possiblity that the Messiah will be looking for perfection when He arrives. This study has been unable to find evidence of any perfect human existing at this time. Therefore, each living person needs to be covered by perfection in order to be judged by the Mahdi or Messiah as worthy to join God at His family table. How can this be achieved?

Chapter 6 introduced a severely stained shirt. If perfect blood was available to cover the imperfect stains, then technically, the shirt is restored to perfection because there is no imperfection found on the shirt. The imperfections of blueberry, coffee, and grass stains are no longer visible. The precisely machined buttons are perfect, the precisely machined stitching is perfect, and the bloodstain is perfect. Absent any imperfection, the shirt qualifies as perfect. It is acceptable before God and can be worn at His family table in paradise. The shirt does not need to be sneaked in through the front door, but instead, a person can walk right in wearing it. Life must be sacrificed to provide the blood, and the blood must be perfect. As discussed earlier, it seems to make sense that the pre-Qur'an Arabs would have been aware of this sacrificial process. Even in the absence of the Bible (the Book), the Qur'an speaks of Adam and Eve and their desire to cover their sin-stained bodies. According to Surahs 7:22 and 20:121, something living had to die to cover them. Living leaves in God's

---

[102]   F. E. Peters, *The Children of Abraham* (Princeton, NJ: Princeton University Press, 2004), 25.

[103]   Hal Lindsey, *The Everlasting Hatred* (Washington, DC: WND Books, 2011), 13.

living garden were sacrificed. In the absence of imperfection, the sacrifice would not have been necessary, and innocent life would have been preserved. The penalty was death to something living. This penalty has not changed.

It is worth taking another closer look at the balancing scale between good compared to bad. As already stated, a penalty exists for the bad, no matter how much good weighs in balance. The wrong is an imperfection and cannot cross into perfection. It was briefly mentioned before, but consider again the traffic violation. Failing to stop at a red light is in violation of the law. Even children who have never studied for a driver's license know this to be true. Offenders will be prosecuted by the law. An offender can stand before the judge and expound on all the good deeds they perform, but the judge will invoke the penalty regardless. The only ransom for the offender is if someone else pays the penalty for them. Redemption can be achieved in that manner, but the penalty must be paid. Imagine a judge stating, "I am in a good mood today. Last night I won the $100 billion lottery. I only came in this morning to tender my notice of resignation and to do something nice for someone before I vacate my position. I have nothing to do tonight, so I am going to spend the night in jail for this offender, plus I will pay the offender's $500 fine. The debt and the stain on their record have now been covered." The judge substituted himself in the place of the offender. He sacrificed his money and leisure. At the time Adam and Eve incurred their penalty, there was no one else to substitute for them. Their stain had to be covered by leaves and those leaves had life. That life was sacrificed when the leaves were detached from their life sustaining source in order to provide the covering as recorded in Surah 7:22 and Genesis 3:7.

Chapter 4 introduced Professor Sachedina's view to a world without oppression. It is a noble virtue. The same recognition belongs to Sheikh Kabbani for his attention to a need for the Mahdi's soon return in order to procure peace throughout humanity. Both seem to imply a twofold prerequisite of universal submission to Islam and elimination of those in opposition. Would the ends justify the means? Will infants born subsequent to the Mahdi's return no longer require correcting? Will doing right come to them naturally? Will the words *mine* and *no* cease to be two of the first words infants speak? Even if that were to happen, what about the sin already commited by those who have reached adulthood by the time the Mahdi arrives? The instruction contained in Surah 64:8 says, "Believe in . . . the Light We have sent down." *Sent*, the past tense of the word *send,* indicates something already accomplished. In other words, the Light that had existed among mankind will return. Imperfection cannot exist in the presence of perfection. Surah 66:8 pleads, "Make perfect for us our light." When the light of the Mahdi arrives, the darkness of imperfection will be eradicated. Those still alive must somehow be made perfect prior to the Mahdi's arrival. How is that achieved?

It was submitted in chapter 8 that the likelihood of success for a forced world peace is greatly hindered. There is another option for anyone willing to consider it. It begins at the infant level and continues as a child develops into a valued citizen. It involves being concerned with the needs of all mankind. As it has unfolded in this study, such a process starts with the manifestation of God in the heart of each parent. The manner in which God operates through mankind is demonstrated throughout the Old Testament. It elaborates on the lives of the names cherished in the Qur'an as well. There are a number of good studies written to help, but reading the Old Testament is always preferred. Even the Qur'an gives recognition to "the Book." However, the method by which a person's heart can absorb and retain God's heart is articulated in the New Testament. It is paraphrased in chapter 6 for the reader's consideration. The related process to reconciliation is found in God's last will and testament.

How can the combination of a substitute person to pay the penalty and provide a perfect covering be achieved? "According to the Qur'an, the descendants of Abraham were chosen by God to bring the 'will of God' to the peoples of the nations.'[104]" The person associated with bringing another person's will is customarily referred to as the *executor*. It would appear that Abraham's descendants would be the executor of God's will. In Genesis 15:4, God notified Abram that "your heir . . . will come forth from your own body." God then set the stage for the eventual fulfillment of His will. He confirmed it in Genesis 17:7 by stating, "I will establish My covenant between Me and you and your descendants . . . throughout their generations for an everlasting covenant, to be God to you and to your descendants after you." How is God's will recognized? An illustration is provided in the next paragraph.

Ordinarily, a parent instinctively protects their child without regard to their own life. They are willing to die for their child. Being a parent, God is no different. As established in the Qur'an and Bible, God possesses the perfection that can cover mankind's imperfections. He alone is innocent, and He alone is judge. He is the only judge that can pay the penalty for mankind. According to this study, covering of imperfections requires sacrifice of life. Ultimately, the covering must be inherently perfect. To die for His children, God had to become something that can lose its life. For the purpose of saving His children, God made Himself a man on earth while also remaining as God in Heaven. In the book of Acts 17:31, the Resurrection of Jesus was submitted as the culminating proof that this had occurred despite mankind's limited ability to fully understand how God could be 100 percent God and 100 percent man. Many times people accept that certain things exist despite their inability to understand how and why. Infinity is a good example of this. Imagine a person begins to shrink and never stops shrinking. What makes sense is that they would eventually disappear. But that is impossible because no matter how small the person shrinks to, they would still be able to see their belly button. They have not disappeared. Consider another simple example. Most people do not know how to design the space shuttle, and they do not know how to

---

[104] *Wikipedia, the free encyclopedia*, s.v. "Islam," accessed April 2013, *http://en.wikipedia.org/wiki/Islam.html*; Momem, "Islam" (1987), 176; *Encyclopædia Britannica Online*.

fly it. This does not prevent the space shuttle from flying. God is infinitely more complex than a belly button or the space shuttle. Being all-powerful and all-knowing, God could have presented Himself to mankind as God the Father, God the Son, God the Holy Ghost, and God the Space Shuttle if He had wanted to. He could have presented Himself in any way He desired. Who could have prevented Him? Nonetheless, in His person and character of Jesus, God was able to, once and for all, provide the perfect sacrifice. His blood paid the fine, and as He served their time in jail for them, Jesus proclaimed His victory to the guilty parties already there (1 Peter 3:19).[105] The analogy is that both the fine and jail time for each traffic violation ever committed have already been settled. This is what the Messiah has achieved. It is a gift from the eternal judge to each offender. But like any other gift, the intended recipient is not forced to receive it. If a gift is forced upon someone, it most likely will not be received in their heart. Bitterness results, and estrangement settles in.

Though thoughts are intangible and occur in the mind, they have a direct effect on the tangible components of mankind's physical makeup. A person's mind can make them sick. If this were not so, the medical field would not be treating people for depression. If this were not true, men and women would not be aroused by the sight of one who appeals to them. Their thoughts result in a visible physical change in a specific body part, and procreation is possible. The mind can cause both positive and negative physical manifestations. If the mind can make a person ill, the mind can also prevent healing. It makes sense that the reverse is also true. In other words, healing begins in the mind. The human heart directly affects the mind. This was demonstrated in chapter 6 with the example of a broken heart. Therefore, both sickness and healing begin in the heart. Taking this to its conclusion, restoring imperfection back to perfection must begin in the heart. Chapter 6 also discussed how the perfect God can be

---

[105] Jay P. Green Sr., *The Interlinear Bible*, Hebrew-Greek-English, 2nd ed. (Peabody, MA: Hendrickson, 1986); Wesley J. Perschbacher, *The New Analytical Greek Lexicon* (Peabody, MA: Hendrickson Publishers, 1990); William MacDonald, *Believer's Bible Commentary* (Nashville, TN: Thomas Nelson, 1995), 2272.

invited into a person's heart. Once in their heart, healing from estrangement begins. As individual family members heal, the dysfunctioning of the family will heal.

It is presumed that someone reading or listening to this book is hoping to remedy disharmony in their family or with friends. This study would recommend that such a person reread chapter 6 and start by inviting Jesus as God into their heart. If this is not acceptable to the reader, the ideas that follow can help either way.

Read and carefully consider the insight offered in *Unlocking Your Family Patterns: Finding Freedom from a Hurtful Past* published by Moody Publishers. It was published in the past as *Secrets of Your Family Tree* and is authored in the unity of Dr. Henry Cloud, Dr. John Townsend, Dr. Earl Henslin, and Dave Carder. A reader or listener does not need to agree with the authors' beliefs to gain ideas and tools to help their family situation. For example,

> A bond between two people is an emotional and personal investment . . . in which . . . feelings, needs, thoughts, values, beliefs, joys, and sorrows—are shared with and valued by another . . . When we are bonded, we "matter" to someone . . . we feel that we make a difference . . . that our presence is desired . . . missed when we are absent . . . in direct contrast to feeling overlooked, forgotten, or even simply tolerated . . . the family should be the very first place where its members can learn to count on the safe nurturance of others to fuel their emotional needs . . . where needs for love are met so that its members . . . go out . . . and take their place as people with purpose and mission. These needs . . . are met through many sorts of experiences:

- Entering the world of the other person and actively listening to what he is saying.

- Understanding the members' needs and emotions and drawing them out, rather than staying on a "task" or "activity" level in all conversations.
- Making vulnerability and need a good thing in the family, so that it's okay to ask for comfort and support.
- Parents modeling vulnerability with each other, so that the kids can see how it's done.[106]

Often, in order to survive the sense of loneliness and emptiness brought on by bonding deficits, individuals develop barriers to intimacy that soothe the pain but prevent the problem from being resolved . . . We . . . come . . . out of the womb . . . empty, frightened, needy beings. We want love. But after repeatedly being punished for having needs, seeing others withdraw from our needs, and having our trust betrayed, most of us inwardly decide that numbness is the best policy: *To protect myself, I must live without needing others. And to live without needing others, I must not feel my own needs.*[107]

In a healthy family the worth of each individual is continually affirmed, even in failure. No one should ever be seen as worthless or all bad . . . grace . . . never condemns or uses anger as a way to point out failure . . . The biblically based family . . . communicates safety and acceptance . . . It creates an atmosphere in which badness, worth, and acceptance are not denied. Badness is called what it is, but the value of the person is affirmed through love.[108]

---

[106] Dave Carder et al., *Unlocking Your Family Patterns* (Chicago, IL: Moody Publishers, 1991, 1993, 2011), 122, 123.

[107] Dave Carder et al., *Unlocking Your Family Patterns* (Chicago, IL: Moody Publishers, 1991, 1993, 2011), 126, 127.

[108] Dave Carder et al., *Unlocking Your Family Patterns* (Chicago, IL: Moody Publishers, 1991, 1993, 2011), 166.

The rebellious child may look at first glance as though he is not being controlled by authority, but in reality he is, since his every action is ruled by his reaction to that authority.[109]

Yuki Hayashi offered some sensible tips found in *Canadian Living*. "If you did the cutting of ties . . . ask yourself if you made a good decision . . . If you did the cutting of ties, remind yourself why . . . Draft a letter . . . hold onto it for 24 hours . . . read it again . . . wait for a response. Don't follow-up via phone or email . . . Hope for the best but prepare for the worst."[110]

This study would also recommend a careful reading of the insight offered in *The Racial and Cultural Divide*. It is published by Tate Publishing & Enterprises and authored by Dr. Cedrick D. Brown. A reader or listener does not need to agree with the author's beliefs to access ideas and tools to help their family situation. The reader will gain a better understanding as to why there are so many media reports that reflect an increase of global violence and hostilities. For example, "If we continue to choose to live in our cultural and racial silos, we are living lives that are faithless, immorally excellent, ignorant, out of control, permissible, ungodly, unkind, and unloving . . . Let's face it; we're different! But there's nothing wrong with this. A Perfect God created us this way, which makes it *all* right!"[111]

In conclusion, there are several books and professional counselors to address family dysfunctions, and others to address world politics and belief systems. What appears to have been overlooked is a faith-based submission

---

[109] Dave Carder et al., *Unlocking Your Family Patterns* (Chicago, IL: Moody Publishers, 1991, 1993, 2011), 183.

[110] Yuki Hayashi, "Estranged: Should you reconnect with an estranged family member?" *Canadian Living*, http://www.canadianliving.com/relationships/family_connections/estranged_should_you_reconnect_with_an_estranged_family_member.php.

[111] Cedrick Brown, *The Racial and Cultural Divide* (Mustang, OK: Tate, 2009), 134, 141.

to suggest that world affairs, belief systems, and family dysfunction might be more related than anyone seems to realize. If indeed they are related, then it stands to reason that as dysfunctions in families are healed, their respective communities will heal. As communities are restored, ultimately nations will be healed. The restoration of nations will, in turn, heal international affairs. Healing such as this can occur even within the estranged family of Abraham's God. The executor has revealed God's will, and healing occurs in response to God's perfection. It is up to each individual to either receive their inheritance or reject it. J. Grathmore Stratus III respects that each person is going to believe what they want to believe. He is in no position to tell anyone what they should believe. J. Grathmore has no desire to insist that anyone believe anything they do not want to believe. However, the author does hope that at least one estranged family will begin the healing process because of what has been shared in this study. Each reader and listener is therefore reminded of the following: "Choose for yourselves today."[112]

J. Grathmore Stratus III extends his gratitude to each reader and listener who has taken time to consider the study presented in *The Estranged Family of Abraham's God*.

Thank you.

---

[112]   Joshua 24:15, the Bible.

BIBLIOGRAPHY

Sources from which extractions have been borrowed for this book are cited fully in the footnotes. Otherwise, this bibliography captures all documentation researched to ensure an objective and reliable presentation of subject matter discussed. The hope is to equip the readers to formulate as informed a conclusion as they possibly can, on their own. Sources were chosen to ensure objectivity. This author makes no claim(s) to agree or disagree with anything found in these sources. In respect of (and for) the three major faith systems that descend from Abraham, side-by-side bilingual/parallel English with Arabic and/or Hebrew and/or Greek references were utilized. This is especially true regarding each respective faith's holy and sacred writings.

"Abrahamic religions." *Wikipedia, the free encyclopedia*. Accessed April 2013. http://en.wikipedia/wiki/Abrahamic_religions.htm.

Ali, Ahmed. *AL-QUR'AN* (bilingual ed.). Princeton, NJ: Princeton University Press, 1993.

The American Heritage Dictionary of the English Language. 4th ed. Houghton Mifflin Company, 2000, 2009.

"Arab." *Wikipedia, the free encyclopedia*. Accessed April 2013. http://en.wikipedia.org/wiki/Arab.html.

"Arabia." *The Free Dictionary*. Accessed March 2013. http://www.thefreedictionary.com/Arabia.html.

Arnold, B. and B. Beyer. *Encountering the Old Testament*. Grand Rapids, MI: Baker, 1999.

"Bible Timeline." http://bibletimeline.info.

Bjornstad, James et al. "Christianity, Cults & Religions" (folded mini-chart 404X). Torrance, CA:
Rose Publishing, 1996, 2000.

Boatwright, Mary T. *Hadrian and the Cities of the Roman Empire*. Princeton, NJ: Princeton University Press, 2000.

Brand, Chad et al. *Holman Illustrated Bible Dictionary*. Nashville, TN: Holman Bible Publishers, 2003.

Brown, Cedrick. *The Racial and Cultural Divide*. Mustang, OK: Tate, 2009.

Brown, Francis et al. *Hebrew and English Lexicon*. Peabody, MA: Hedrickson, 2001.

Caner, M. and E. Caner. *Unveiling Islam*. Grand Rapids, MI: Kregel, 2002.

Carder, Dave et al. *Unlocking Your Family Patterns*. Chicago, IL: Moody Publishers, 1991, 1993, 2011.

Catherwood, Christopher. *Christians, Muslims and Islamic Rage.* Grand Rapids, MI: Zondervan, 2003.

"A Chart of Infant Behaviors." Accessed September 2013. http://www.cog. brown.edu/courses.cg63/ChartOfInfantBehaviors.htm.

"Circumstances Surrounding Muhammed's Death." *WikiIslam.* Accessed April 2013. http://WikiIslam.net/Wiki/circumstances_Surrounding_ Muhammed's_Death.html.

"Collateral." *The Free Dictionary.* Accessed March 2013. http://www. thefreedictionary.com/collateral.html.

Collins English Dictionary—Complete and Unabridged. HarperCollins Publishers, 1991, 1994, 1998, 2000, 2003.

"Comparison of Islam, Judaism and Christianity" (chart). In *RELIGIONFACTS,* September 2013. http://www.religionfacts.com/islam/comparison_charts/ islam_judaism_christianity.htm.

DeHann, Martin R., II. *When East Meets West.* Grand Rapids, MI: RBC Ministries, 2003.

Driver, S. R. and A. D. Neubauer. *The Fifty-Third Chapter of Isaiah According to Jewish Interpreters.* Oxford and London: Parker, 1877.

Eisenberg, A., H. E. Murkoff, and S. E. Hathaway. *What to Expect the First Year.* New York: Workman Publishing, 1989.

Elwell, W. and R. Yarbrough. *Encountering the New Testament.* 2nd ed. Grand Rapids, MI: Baker, 1998.

"Estranged." *The Free Dictionary*. Accessed March 2013. http://www.thefreedictionary.com/estranged.html.

"Estranged." *Wiktionary, the free dictionary*. Accessed March 2013. http://en.wiktionary.org/wiki/estranged.html.

"Estranged: Should you reconnect with an estranged family member?" In *Canadian Living,* March 2013. http://www.canadianliving.com/relationships/family_connections/estranged_should_you_reconnect_with_an_estranged_family_member.php.

"Executor." *Wikipedia, the free encyclopedia*. Accessed September 2013. http://en.wikipedia.org/wiki/Executor.html.

"Family." *Wikipedia, the free encyclopedia*. Accessed March 2013. https://en.wikipedia.org/wiki/Family.html.

Farlex. "Arabia." *The Free Dictionary*. May 2013. http:///thefreedictionary.com/Arabia.html.

Framingham, Jane. "What is Psychological Assessment?" September 2013. http://psychcentral.com/lib/what-is-psychological-assessment/0005890.

Geisler, Norman L. and Frank Turek. *I Don't Have Enough Faith to Be an Atheist*. Wheaton, IL:
Crossway Books, 2004.

Ghattas, R. and C. Ghattas. *A Christian Guide to the Qur'an*. Grand Rapids, MI: Kregel, 2009.

Giamba, Bruno R. "Let's Get Real." Sermon in Souderton, Pennsylvania, August 2013.

"God." *Merriam-Webster.* Accessed April 2013. http://merriam-webster.com/dictionary/god.

"God." *Wikipedia, the free encyclopedia.* Accessed April 2013. http://en.wikipedia.org/wiki/God.html.

Goriss, Luana. "Jewish Contributions to Society." *About.com.* Accessed March 2013. http://judaism.about.com/od/culture/a/contribution.htm.

Green, Jay P., Sr. *The Interlinear Bible.* Hebrew-Greek-English. 2nd ed. Peabody, MA:
Hendrickson, 1986.

Hadas, Moses. *Complete Works of Tacitus.* New York, NY: Random House, 1942.

Hayashi, Yuki. "Estranged: Should you reconnect with an estranged family member?" In *Canadian Living.* http://www.canadianliving.com/relationships/family_connections/estranged_should_you_reconnect_with_an_estranged_family_member.php.

"Hebrew." *The Free Dictionary.* Accessed March 2013. http://www.thefreedictionary.com/Hebrew.html.

Hutchings, Noah W. "A Letter from the Pastor." Bethany, OK: Southwest Radio Ministries, July 2013.

Idara Dawat-O-Irshad. "Identification of the Promised Messiah." August 2013. http://www.irshad.org/islam/prophecy/messiah.htm.

"Ishmael." *The Free Dictionary*. Accessed September 2013. http://www.thefreedictionary.com/Ishmael.html.

"Ishmael." *Wikipedia, the free encyclopedia*. Accessed September 2013. http://en.wikipedia.org/wiki/Ishmael.

"Islam." *Wikipedia, the free encyclopedia*. Accessed April 2013. http://en.wikipedia.org/wiki/Islam.html.

"Islamic Contributions to Medieval Europe." *Wikipedia, the free encyclopedia*. Accessed March 2013. http://en.wikipedia.org/wiki/Islamic_contributions_to_Medieval_Europe.html.

"Islamic Golden Age." *Wikipedia, the free encyclopedia*. Accessed April 2013. http://en.wikipedia.org/wiki/Islamic_Golden_Age.

"Jews." *Wikipedia, the free encyclopedia*. Accessed April 2013. http://en.wikipedia.org/wiki/Jews.html.

"Judaism." *Wikipedia, the free encyclopedia*. Accessed April 2013. http://en.wikipedia.org/wiki/Judaism.html.

La Vista Church of Christ. "Where is Edom Today?" 2003, 2013. http://lavistachurchofchrist.org/LVanswers/2005/09-24.htm.

LeBey, Barbara. *Family Estrangements*. Atlanta, GA: Longstreet Press, 2001.

Life Application Study Bible. Wheaton, IL: Tyndale House Publishers, 1991.

"Lineal." *The Free Dictionary*. Accessed August 2013. http://www.thefreedictionary.com/lineal.html.

Lindsey, Hal. *The Everlasting Hatred.* Washington, DC: WND Books, 2011.

MacDonald, William. *Believer's Bible Commentary.* Nashville, TN: Thomas Nelson, 1995.

"The Mahdi: Islam's Awaited Messiah." August 2013. http://www.answering-islam.org/Authors/JR/Future/ch04_the_mahdi.htm.

Mead, Frank et al. *Handbook of Denomination in the United States* (20th ed.). Nashville, TN: Abington, 1985.

Meyers, Allen C. *The Eerdmans Bible Dictionary*. Grand Rapids, MI: Wm. B. Eerdmans, 1987.

The Modern Library—New York. *Complete Works of Tacitus.* Modern Library College Editions. Distributed by McGraw-Hill Inc. New York, NY: Random House, 1942.

"Mohammed, Initial Revelations and Relationships." In *30-Days Prayer Network*. Accessed May 12, 2013. http://www.30-days.net/islam/history/mohammed-revelations-relationships.html.

Muncaster, Ralph O. *Can You Trust the Bible?* Eugene, OR: Harvest House Publishers, 2000.

Muncaster, Ralph O. *How Do We Know Jesus Is God?* Eugene, OR: Harvest House Publishers, 2000.

Muncaster, Ralph O. *Is the Bible Really a Message from God?* Eugene, OR: Harvest House Publishers, 2000.

Muncaster, Ralph O. *What Is the Proof for the Resurrection?* Eugene, OR: Harvest House Publishers, 2000.

"Muslim." *Wikipedia, the free encyclopedia.* Accessed April 2013. http://en.wikipedia.org/wiki/Muslim.html.

National Center for Infants, Toddlers, and Families. "ZERO TO THREE—Behavior & Development" (Washington, DC: September 2013). http://www.zerotothree.org/child-development.

Nelson, Eric. *The Roman Empire.* Indianapolis, IN: Alpha Books, 2002.

Nelson, Thomas. *The Three-In-One Bible Reference Companion.* Nashville, TN: Thomas Nelson Publishers, 1982.

New American Standard Bible (bilingual ed.). Anaheim, CA: Foundation Publications, 1960.

The Ohio State University (Wexner Medical Center). "Comprehensive Psychiatric Evaluations." In *About Mental Health*, September 2013. http://medicalcenter.osu.edu/patientcare/healthcare_services/mental_health/mental_health_about/about_mental_health/comprehensive_psychiatric_evaluations/Pages/index.aspx.

"Palestine." *Columbia Encyclopedia.* Accessed September 2013. http://www.answers.com/topic/palestine.

"Palestine." *Gale Encyclopedia of the Mideast & N. Africa.* Accessed September 2013. http://www.answers.com/topic/palestine.

Perschbacher, Wesley J. *The New Analytical Greek Lexicon.* Peabody, MA: Hendrickson Publishers, 1990.

Peters, F. E. *The Children of Abraham.* Princeton, NJ: Princeton University Press, 2004.

Peters, Joan. *From Time Immemorial.* Chicago, IL: JKAP, 1984.

Randolph, Mary J. D. "What Does an Executor Do?" In *NOLO Law for ALL.* Accessed September 2013. nolo.com/legal-encyclopedia/what-does-executor-do-30236.html.

"Reason for the Delay in the Burial of the Prophet." In *Islamweb* (English), April 2013. http://Islamweb.net.html.

Richardson, Don. *Secrets of the Koran.* Ventura, CA: Regal, 2003.

Ridenour, Fritz. *So What's the Difference?* Ventura, CA: Regal, 1967.

Rizvi, Syed Saeed Akhtar. "The Life of Muhammad the Prophet." April 2013. http://Al-Islam.org/lifeprophet.html.

Rudd, Steve. "The Edomites." http://www.bible.ca/archeology/bible-archeology-edomite-territory-mt-seir.htm.

Sells, Michael. *Approaching the Quran.* 2nd ed. Ashland, OR: White Cloud, 1999.

"Semitic people." *Wikipedia, the free encyclopedia.* Accessed April 2013. http://en.wikipedia.org/wiki/Semitic_people.html.

Shakir, M. H., trans. *Concordance of the Qur'an*. Elmhurst, NY: Tahrike Tarsile Qur'an, 2005.

Silas. "The Death of Muhammad." April 2013. http://answering-islam/Silas/mo-death.htm.

Spargimino, Larry. "The Hostile Religion of Atheism." In *Prophetic Observer* volume 18 (October 2011): 4. Bethany, Oklahoma.

Speller, Elizabeth. *Following Hadrian*. New York, NY: Oxford University Press, 2003.

Spencer, Robert. *The Politically Incorrect Guide to Islam and the Crusades*. Washington, DC:
Regnery, 2005.

Strobel, Lee. *The Case for Christ*. Grand Rapids, MI: Zondervan, 1998.

Strong, James. *Strong's Exhaustive Concordance of the Bible*. Peabody, MA: Hedrickson [undated].

"Timeline of the Prophets." 3 Dj I; Qa'daj 1434 AH. Sunday, September 8, 2013. http://www.themeaningofislam.org/prophets/overview/timeline.html.

Tyson, Jerry. "Vatican Shake-Up—World Wake-Up." In *Prophetic Observer* volume 20 (March 2013): 4. Bethany, Oklahoma.

US National Library of Medicine, National Institutes of Health (NIH). "MedlinePlus—Child Behavior Disorders." September 2013. http://www.nim.nih.gov/medlineplus/childbehaviordisorders.html.

Van Impe, Jack. "World Report." In *Perhaps Today*. Troy, MI: JVI Ministries, May-June 2013.

Van Impe, Jack. "World Report." In *Perhaps Today*. Troy, MI: JVI Ministries, September-October 2013.

Wasalem, Wallah u Aalam. "Is This the Grave of Prophet Muhammed (Peace Be Upon Him)?"
May 2013. http://.oocities.org/mkamranparacha/ISGraveofProphetSAW.htm (This page is an outdated, user-generated website brought to you by an archive. It was mirrored from Geocities at the end of October 2009. For any questions about this page, contact the respective author. To report any malicious content send the URL to oocities[at]gmail[dot]com. For any questions concerning the archive, visit our main page: *OoCities.org*.). http://web.archive.org/web/20091026194848/geocities.com/mkamronparacha/ISGraveofProphetSAW.

The Webster's College Dictionary. Random House Inc. 1991, 1997, 2005. K Dictionaries Ltd. 2013.

Whiston, William and Paul L. Maier. *The New Complete Works of Josephus*. Grand Rapids, MI:
Kregel Publications, 1999.

Wood, Bryant G. "What Do Mt. Horeb, The Mountain of God, Mt. Paran and Mt. Seir Have to Do with Mt. Sinai?" http://www.biblearchaeology.org/post/2008/11/What-Do-Mt-Horeb2c-The-Mountain-of-God2c-Mt-Paran-and-Mt-Seir-Have-to-Do-with-Mt-Sinai.aspx.

Wood, David. "Deceptive God, Incompetent Messiah." August 2013. http://www.answering-islam.org/Authors/Wood/deceptive_god.htm.

Youngblood, Ronald F. *Nelson's New Illustrated Bible Dictionary*. Nashville, TN: Thomas Nelson, 1995.

Yourcenar, Marguerite. *Memoirs of Hadrian*. 19 Union Square West, New York:
Farrar, Straus and Giroux, 1974.

INDEX

AUTHOR'S BIOGRAPHY

The author, J. Grathmore Stratus III, was born on the south shore of Long Island in Bay Shore, New York. He was raised in his grandmother's house located directly across the street from busy boat-building and repair yards, as well as passenger terminals and fishermen wharves. Starting at the age of seven, an appreciation for community involvement was sparked by serving in the local junior firemen organization. A rugged appreciation for mountaineering and wild creatures was gained from summer canoeing and hiking in the Adirondack Mountains of New York. Back on Long Island, however, the boys closest to his grandmother's home were all several years older and much bigger. They never seemed to grow weary of targeting this younger, very overweight, bucktoothed, and extremely nearsighted boy. Even the schoolgirls would make fun of him. There was never a shortage of harsh nicknames. The harsh realities of being bullied served as motivation, leading to athletic scholarships, service aboard oceangoing steamships to foreign lands, and an unwavering commitment to serve the local community (and beyond).

A sincere appreciation for other cultures, belief systems, and viewpoints was gained while navigating cargo ships and oil tankers to overseas destinations. Insight gained helped structure J. Grathmore's thoughts for publication in the *Journal of Commerce, Best's Review, Lloyd's List, National Underwriter,*

Fairplay magazine, and other global publications, leading to peer acceptance and personal communication with international market leaders.

J. Grathmore Stratus III holds a bachelor of science degree in the field of international relations and commerce, as well as a bachelor of arts degree in the field of theology. He currently resides outside of Philadelphia, Pennsylvania, in southern New Jersey.

Edwards Brothers Malloy
Thorofare, NJ USA
March 4, 2014